EFFORTLESS ADHD ORGANIZATION

AFFORDABLE LIFE HACKS FOR ADULTS WITH ADHD TO REDUCE STRESS, INCREASE PRODUCTIVITY, & STREAMLINE DECLUTTERING IN LESS THAN 30 MINUTES A DAY

STERLING CHENEY

Copyright © 2024 by Sterling Avery Cheney

All rights reserved.

No portion of this book may be reproduced in any form without written permission from the publisher or author, except as permitted by U.S. copyright law.

This publication is designed to provide accurate and authoritative information in regard to the subject matter covered. It is sold with the understanding that neither the author nor the publisher is engaged in rendering legal, investment, accounting or other professional services. While the publisher and author have used their best efforts in preparing this book, they make no representations or warranties with respect to the accuracy or completeness of the contents of this book and specifically disclaim any implied warranties of merchantability or fitness for a particular purpose. No warranty may be created or extended by sales representatives or written sales materials. The advice and strategies contained herein may not be suitable for your situation. You should consult with a professional when appropriate. Neither the publisher nor the author shall be liable for any loss of profit or any other commercial damages, including but not limited to special, incidental, consequential, personal, or other damages.

Book Cover by Distinguish
Illustrations by Unissa J Utami
1st edition 2024

First, to my loving wife. You've encouraged me through every stage of this project, no matter how time consuming or stressful. You are my light.

Second, to Greg Denning, the man who's changed my relationship with books - and the mentors inside them - forever. Thank you.

CONTENTS

Introduction   9

PART I
Laying the Foundations for ADHD-Friendly Organization

Chapter 1.1   15
Understanding ADHD and Its Impact on Organization

Chaper 1.2   19
Setting Up Your Mindset for Success: Overcoming Procrastination

Chapter 1.3   25
Essential Tools and Apps for Staying Organized with ADHD

Chapter 1.4   31
Creating a Personalized Organizational System That Works for You

Chapter 1.5   37
Short Sessions: Organizing Tasks into Manageable Chunks

Chapter 1.6   43
The Importance of Routine: Building Consistency in Daily Life

PART II
Digital Decluttering and Management

Chapter 2.1   51
Identifying and Eliminating Digital Clutter

Chapter 2.2   57
Organizing Your Digital Files: A Step-by-Step Guide

Chapter 2.3   61
Email Management Hacks for Quick Wins

Chapter 2.4   67
Streamlining Your Social Media Interactions

Chapter 2.5   73
Using Technology to Automate Organization

Chapter 2.6   77
Protecting Your Digital Space: Tips and Tools

PART III
Home Organization: Room-by-Room Strategies

Chapter 3.1 — 85
The Kitchen: Simplifying Meal Prep and Storage

Chapter 3.2 — 91
The Living Room: Maintaining Order in Shared Spaces

Chapter 3.3 — 97
The Bedroom: Creating a Calm and Organized Retreat

Chapter 3.4 — 103
The Bathroom: Quick Cleans and Efficient Storage

Chapter 3.5 — 109
The Home Office: Maximizing Productivity

Chapter 3.6 — 115
The Garage and Storage Areas: Keeping Clutter at Bay

PART IV
Managing Time and Tasks Efficiently

Chapter 4.1 — 123
Understanding Time Blindness in ADHD

Chapter 4.2 — 127
Time Blocking: A Visual Method for Managing Daily Tasks

Chapter 4.3 — 133
The Art of Prioritization: What to Do and When

Chapter 4.4 — 139
Overcoming Overwhelm: Techniques to Break Down Large Projects

Chapter 4.5 — 145
The Pomodoro Technique: Tailored for ADHD

Chapter 4.6 — 151
Setting Realistic Goals and Celebrating Small Victories

Chapter 4.7 — 157
Avoiding Common Time Management Pitfalls

PART V
ADHD and Family Life

Chapter 5.1 — 165
Organizing Family Activities with Ease

Chapter 5.2 — 171
ADHD-Friendly Strategies for Managing Children's Schedules

Chapter 5.3 — 177
Creating ADHD-Inclusive Family Routines

Chapter 5.4 — 183
Decluttering with Kids: Making It Fun and Engaging

Chapter 5.5 — 189
Managing Family Expectations and Responsibilities

Chapter 5.6 — 195
Coping with Multi-Tasking Challenges in Family Life

PART VI
ADHD in the Workplace

Chapter 6.1 — 205
Organizing Your Work Desk for Maximum Efficiency

Chapter 6.2 — 209
Handling Work-Related Stress with Organizational Techniques

Chapter 6.3 — 215
Navigating Office Politics and Interpersonal Relationships

Chapter 6.4 — 221
Time Management Tips for Meetings and Deadlines

Chapter 6.5 — 227
Creating an ADHD-Friendly Workflow

Chapter 6.6 — 233
Career Advancement: Leveraging Organizational Skills for Success

PART VII
Lifestyle Organization: From Daily Routines to Special Events

Chapter 7.1 — 241
Organizing Personal Projects and Hobbies

Chapter 7.2 — 247
Streamlining Your Social Life: Events and Outings

Chapter 7.3 — 253
Travel Made Easy: Packing and Planning Tips

Chapter 7.4 — 259
Balancing Social and Personal Time Effectively

Chapter 7.5 — 265
Seasonal Organizing: Adjusting Your Space and Schedule

Chapter 7.6 — 271
Maintaining a Minimalist Lifestyle with ADHD

PART VIII
Advanced Organizing Challenges and Solutions

Chapter 8.1 — 279
Long-Term Projects: Staying Organized from Start to Finish

Chapter 8.2 — 285
Organizing Financial Documents ADHD-Friendly

Chapter 8.3 — 291
Overcoming the Challenges of Hyperfocus in Organization

Chapter 8.4 — 297
Advanced Labeling and Sorting Techniques

PART IX
Long-Term Success and Continuous Improvement

Chapter 9.1 — 305
Reviewing and Revising Your Organizational Systems

Chapter 9.2 — 309
Staying Motivated: Long-Term Strategies for Organizational Success

Chapter 9.3 — 315
Embracing New Organizational Technologies and Tools

Chapter 9.4 — 321
Dealing with Setbacks and Reorganizing

Chapter 9.5 — 327
Celebrating Your Organizational Achievements

Chapter 9.6 — 333
Future-Proofing Your Organization Skills

'Till We Meet Again — 339
References — 343

INTRODUCTION

Last Tuesday, as I scrambled through the chaos of unwashed dishes, scattered bills, and unsorted emails—each vying for my attention like overly enthusiastic squirrels at a nut convention—I stumbled upon an old notebook buried under a pile of laundry. Flipping through its pages, I rediscovered a series of notes I'd absentmindedly written during similar moments of disorder. These weren't just random notes; they were the seeds of what would become one of my most fulfilling and successful public speeches. It's like finding a winning lottery ticket in the pocket of your winter coat—if only I could remember where I put that coat. This moment of clarity amidst the chaos is not just a fluke—it's the hidden superpower of living with ADHD.

For over a decade, I have navigated the vibrant and often unpredictable waters of a neurodivergent brain. I chose early on to approach ADHD not as a hurdle but as a unique advantage, a different way of seeing the world that, when understood, could be tapped into as a profound source of creativity and energy. It's kind of like being handed a Swiss Army knife with way too many tools

—sure, it's confusing, but boy, can it do some amazing stuff if you figure it out! I steered clear of medication, not out of disdain, but from a deep desire to fully engage with the intrinsic nature of my mind and leverage it to its fullest.

This book is born from that journey. It's crafted for you—the young adults in the throes of starting families or carving out careers, who might find the traditional methods of organization not only inadequate but frustrating. Think of this book as your personal tour guide through the jungle of ADHD, complete with a machete for cutting through the underbrush of daily distractions. Here, I offer not just tips but a new way to think about organizing life when you have ADHD. These are practical, affordable, and, most importantly, tailored strategies to help you streamline your daily life in less than 30 minutes a day.

You won't find generic advice here. Each page is filled with visually engaging, easy-to-implement solutions specifically designed for the ADHD mind. It's like a recipe book for chaos control—with less soufflé and more survival. From conquering digital clutter to balancing family life and career demands, this book covers it all. It's not just a guide; it's an interactive toolkit. You'll find personal stories of triumph, visual aids, and checklists that transform reading into action.

I understand the tug-of-war between societal expectations and personal reality that so many of us face. Society says, "Clean desk," but your brain says, "Creative explosion." This book acknowledges those challenges and casts a vision of hope and practical change. It's a testament that with the right approach, transforming daily chaos into a productive, organized lifestyle isn't just a lofty goal—it's achievable.

I invite you not just to read this book but to use it. Stuff a cork in the librarian who lives in your head! Books are meant to be consumed and experienced. Please write in the margins, smell the paper, spill some coffee on it, fill out the checklists, reference the built-in dog-eared pages, and fully engage with the strategies laid out. Let this be *more* than a reading experience—a turning point!

Together, let's redefine what it means to live efficiently with ADHD. Embrace the quirks, harness the energy, and make this a journey worth laughing about. With the right tools, your neurodivergent brain is not a barrier but a beacon guiding you to a more organized, fulfilling life. Let's start this journey together, right now.

PART I

LAYING THE FOUNDATIONS FOR ADHD-FRIENDLY ORGANIZATION

Have you ever found yourself searching for your keys in the refrigerator, or maybe discovering that missing sock in the oven? If this sounds all too familiar, you might just be part of the vibrant ADHD club. My own life seemed like a constant episode of "Where did I put that thing again?" until I realized that my chaotic environment was a mirror of my neurological wiring (and that my wife somehow knew exactly where that "thing" was). This chapter is all about understanding that wiring—embracing it, not fighting it—and laying down the first stones on your path to an organized life that respects your unique brain. Be patient, stay with me, and trust that you *are* capable of understanding how to be, well, you! Fully unlocked and unleashed.

CHAPTER 1.1

UNDERSTANDING ADHD AND ITS IMPACT ON ORGANIZATION

Neurological Insights

ADHD isn't just about occasionally losing your car keys or getting distracted by the next shiny object. At its core, ADHD involves a variety of executive functions—those brain processes that help you plan, organize, strategize, remember details, and manage time. For those with ADHD, these functions can be inconsistent, leading to what is known as executive dysfunction. This doesn't mean you're not smart or capable; think of it more like trying to juggle with one hand tied behind your back—it's possible, just a bit more challenging.

Recent research pinpoints how this dysfunction manifests: difficulty prioritizing tasks, forgetting what you started five minutes ago, or struggling to estimate how long a task will take: "Yeah, I just need to take care of something quick! I'll call you back in 5 minutes..." Meanwhile, "5 minutes later," that family member or friend you were talking to looks bleary-eyed at their ringing phone: it's 11:23 PM, 5 hours since you started the original task.

Traditional organizational strategies often fail to take these quirks into account, leading many with ADHD to feel like square pegs being forced into round holes.

Behavioral Patterns

Now, let's talk behavior. Commonly, you might find yourself surrounded by half-completed tasks, from laundry to paperwork, because starting tasks feels as daunting as climbing Everest. Or perhaps you hyper-focus on a hobby or task well into the night, completely losing track of time. It's these patterns that can disrupt both personal and professional aspects of life, turning everyday duties into Herculean efforts.

The impact extends beyond personal inconvenience. In the workplace, it might look like missed deadlines or forgotten meetings. At home, it can translate into overwhelming clutter or tension with family members over uncompleted tasks.

Emotional Consequences

The chaos of ADHD doesn't stop at physical or behavioral aspects; it has profound emotional repercussions as well. The continual stress of misplaced items missed appointments, or last-minute scrambles can lead to significant anxiety. There's also the frustration of knowing you want to organize or follow through on tasks, but somehow, you just can't make it happen.

Understanding these emotional responses is crucial. It's about acknowledging that frustration and anxiety are not failures but signals. Your emotions are telling you that the traditional methods aren't working, and it's time for a change.

CHAPTER 1.1 | 17

Chapter Checklist

- ☐ Assess your workspace for visual clutter.
- ☐ Set timers for task segmentation.
- ☐ Use color-coded systems for immediate visual feedback.
- ☐ Reflect daily: note what's working and what's not.

Bullet Point Summary

- ADHD impacts key executive functions crucial for organizing daily life, affecting planning, prioritizing, and time management abilities.
- Individuals with ADHD frequently encounter obstacles such as struggling to complete tasks, misplacing items, and losing track of time, which can disrupt both personal and professional life.
- The emotional repercussions of these organizational challenges often manifest as heightened stress and anxiety, contributing to a cycle that further impedes organization and productivity.

CHAPER 1.2

SETTING UP YOUR MINDSET FOR SUCCESS: OVERCOMING PROCRASTINATION

Ah, procrastination—the art of avoiding today what you can stress about tomorrow. If ADHD were a sport, procrastination might just be the national pastime. It's that familiar pull to do anything but the task at hand, even if that means reorganizing your sock drawer by color rather than tackling the mountain of emails awaiting your reply. But what if we could shift that mindset? What if the energy spent avoiding tasks could be channeled into conquering them? This part of our adventure is about rewriting the procrastination narrative and setting up a mindset that understands and outsmarts the procrastination gremlin.

First, let's talk about reframing our mindset. It's about flipping the script from dread to anticipation, from stress to challenge. This is not about sugarcoating the bitter pill of responsibility but about finding genuine value in getting things done. Positive thinking plays a crucial role here. It's like putting on a pair of glasses that turn the grey skies of "I have to" into the blue skies of "I get to." It's about viewing each task as a stepping stone towards your goals, not a hurdle. And self-compassion? Non-negotiable. Remember, berating yourself for not meeting unrealistic expectations is like yelling at a plant to grow faster—ineffective and kind of sad. Instead, nurturing your mind with kind words and realistic goals sets the stage for genuine growth and productivity.

Now, onto building motivation—this is the fuel for our organizational engine. Small, achievable goals are your best friends here. Imagine them as mini checkpoints in a video game; each one you hit gives you a boost and keeps the momentum up. And why not make it enjoyable with some rewards? If your brain is a fan of immediate gratification, use that. Finished a task? Great, you get a five-minute YouTube break or a coffee treat. These little incentives cater to the ADHD brain's reward sensitivity, making you more likely to stick with the task at hand.

Identifying procrastination triggers is like knowing where the booby traps are in an ancient temple. Common culprits include overwhelming tasks, fear of failure, or simply not knowing where to start. Awareness is your torch here. Shine a light on these triggers, and they become less daunting. Break down overwhelming tasks into bite-sized pieces. Afraid of failing? Reframe failures as learning opportunities. Not sure where to start? Just start anywhere—momentum is often more important than direction in the early stages. And if you're anything like me, sometimes the most giant booby trap is just opening the fridge and forgetting why you did it—but hey, at least now you have a snack for the adventure ahead!

Success stories serve as the proof in the pudding. Take Liz, for example, who always put off starting her reports until the eleventh hour. She started sooner with more enthusiasm by setting up a reward system where she treated herself to a smoothie after drafting a report outline. Or consider Mike, who realized his fear of failure was paralyzing him. By acknowledging this fear and reframing his tasks as experiments rather than do-or-die missions, he reduced his procrastination significantly.

Embracing these strategies does not mean transforming into a hyper-organized robot. It's about making peace with your neurodivergent brain, understanding its whims and fancies, and gently steering it towards productivity, one small, rewarding step at a time. I know that tackling procrastination can feel like navigating an ancient temple filled with booby traps, but remember, you've got the torch to light your way. Each small victory is like discovering a hidden treasure, bringing you closer to your goals! As you turn this page, carry with you not just plans for organization, but a renewed mindset that sees procrastination not as a foe, but as a puzzle to be solved, a challenge to be met with creativity and courage.

22 | EFFORTLESS ADHD ORGANIZATION

Chapter Checklist

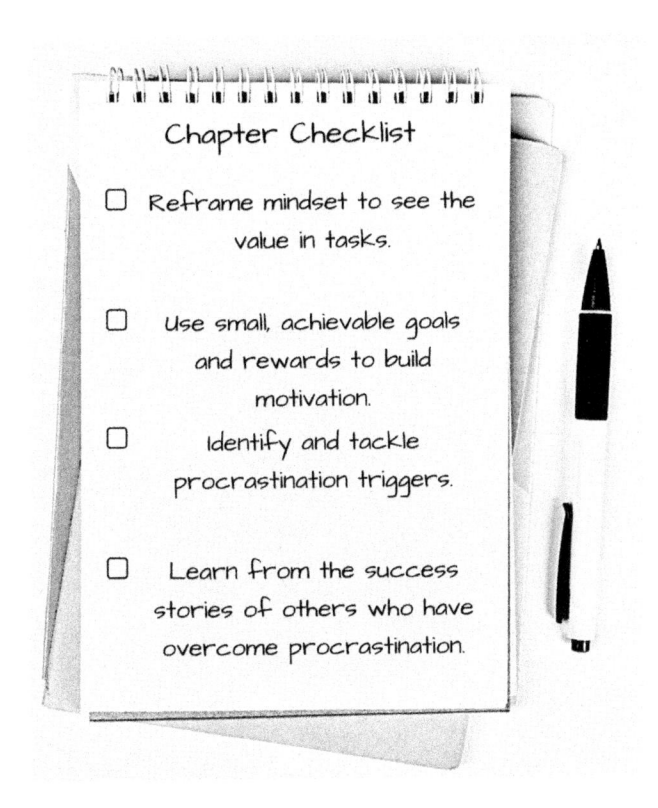

- ☐ Reframe mindset to see the value in tasks.
- ☐ Use small, achievable goals and rewards to build motivation.
- ☐ Identify and tackle procrastination triggers.
- ☐ Learn from the success stories of others who have overcome procrastination.

Bullet Point Summary

- Reframe mindset to see the value in tasks.
- Use small, achievable goals and rewards to build motivation.
- Identify and tackle procrastination triggers.
- Learn from the success stories of others who have overcome procrastination.

CHAPTER 1.3

ESSENTIAL TOOLS AND APPS FOR STAYING ORGANIZED WITH ADHD

Let's face it, the digital age is both a blessing and a curse, especially for those of us with ADHD. On one end, we're bombarded with notifications and distractions. On the other, we have access to some incredibly powerful tools designed to keep our chaotic lives a bit more orderly. Embracing these tools can often mean the difference between feeling overwhelmed and staying on top of your game. For starters, let's dive into the digital arsenal available at our fingertips. Task managers and digital calendars are not just apps, but lifelines for many with ADHD. Take, for instance, apps like Trello or Asana, which allow you to break projects into manageable tasks, set deadlines, and even share your progress with others—perfect for both visual thinkers and those who need a nudge now and then to stay on track.

Then, there are digital calendars like Google Calendar, which can sync across all your devices, ensuring you never miss an important date. What makes these tools particularly handy for folks with ADHD is their ability to send reminders. It's like having a personal assistant who gently taps you on the shoulder, saying, "Hey, remember you have a dentist appointment tomorrow at 3 PM." This feature alone can reduce a significant amount of stress and last-minute scrambling.

Shifting gears to physical tools, there's something inherently grounding about the tactile feel of planners and journals, which digital tools can't completely replicate. Writing down your tasks, events, and deadlines by hand can aid in encoding this information into your memory. For many with ADHD, the act of writing can help focus thoughts and form a more transparent plan of action. Customizable organization systems like a bullet journal can be particularly effective. They combine the elements of a planner, diary, and to-do list, and they can be tailored to one's personal needs—making them an invaluable resource for someone whose brain often runs a marathon of thoughts.

Integration of these tools into daily life is where the real magic happens. It's not just about owning these tools; it's about making them a part of your life. Consistency is key. For instance, setting a specific daily time to update and review your digital planner can solidify this habit. It could be in the morning, as you sip your coffee and brace for the day, or in the evening when you wind down and prepare for tomorrow. Linking tool usage to an already established routine increases the chances that it'll stick.

Of course, for those of us with ADHD, 'consistency' is the ultimate mythical creature—right up there with unicorns and inbox zero. Sure, I *mean* to update my planner every day. Still, somehow, it's always the same scenario: I sit down with my coffee, open the planner app, and 20 minutes later, I'm deep into researching whether penguins have knees. By the time I remember the planner, the coffee's cold, and my to-do list looks like, 'Don't forget to Google penguin knees.' The point is to be nice to yourself, give yourself some grace (especially in the beginning), and keep having the patience to bring your focus back to your tools and to-do lists. That slice of advice goes for every task you undertake while dealing with ADHD!

In terms of recommendations, user feedback from the ADHD community suggests a strong preference for tools that are user-friendly and minimally distracting. For digital tools, Todoist scores high due to its simple interface and powerful task management features. As for physical tools, the classic Moleskine planner remains a favorite for its quality and versatility, allowing for easy adaptations like a bullet journal approach.

Navigating through the myriad of organizational tools available can seem daunting, but finding the right ones that click with your personal and professional life can turn them from mere tools into lifelines. I know you've been putting in so much effort, and I want you to know how proud I am of your determination. Whether digital or physical, the right organizational aids not only keep you on track but also bring a much-needed sense of control and accomplishment. Keep believing in yourself—you've got this, and I'm here to support you every step of the way. As we proceed, remember that these tools are not just about keeping you organized; they're about enhancing your quality of life one well-planned day at a time.

28 | EFFORTLESS ADHD ORGANIZATION

Chapter Checklist

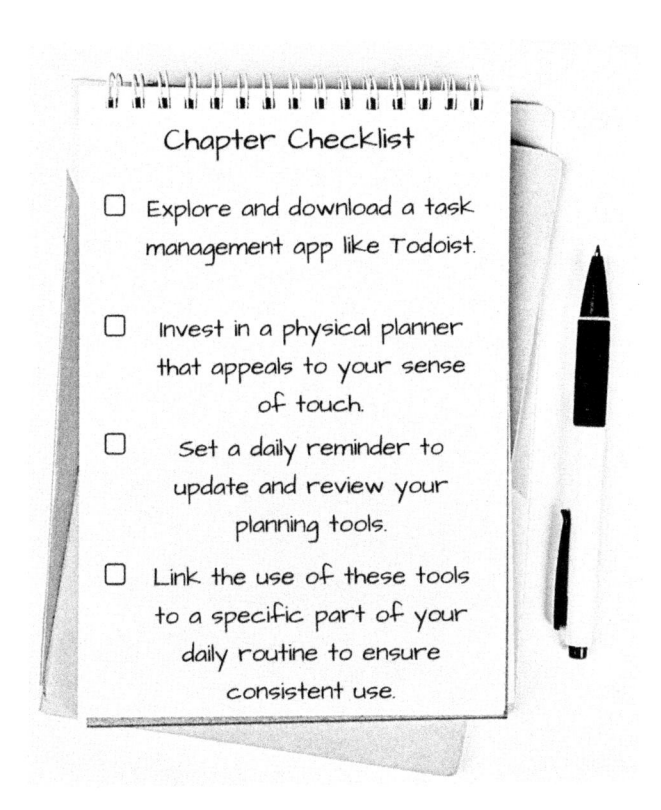

☐ Explore and download a task management app like Todoist.

☐ Invest in a physical planner that appeals to your sense of touch.

☐ Set a daily reminder to update and review your planning tools.

☐ Link the use of these tools to a specific part of your daily routine to ensure consistent use.

Bullet Point Summary

- Digital tools like task managers and calendars are crucial for time and task management.
- Physical tools such as planners aid memory through tactile engagement.
- Integrating these tools into daily routines enhances their effectiveness.
- Community-recommended tools include Todoist for digital and Moleskine planners for physical planning.

CHAPTER 1.4

CREATING A PERSONALIZED ORGANIZATIONAL SYSTEM THAT WORKS FOR YOU

If you've ever felt like the conventional one-size-fits-all organizational systems are more of a straitjacket than a tool for freedom, you're not alone. Many with ADHD find that these systems don't accommodate the unique way their brain operates. Instead of forcing yourself to adapt to these pre-made solutions, why not craft a system that bends to your will, one that grooves with your life's rhythms and quirks? Crafting a personalized organizational system isn't just about making lists or buying bins; it's about creating a space that feels like a backstage pass to your most productive self, tailored to the concert of your life.

First, let's explore personalization strategies. The cornerstone of any effective personal and organizational system is that it must reflect your lifestyle, your personal preferences, and the specific challenges posed by your ADHD. This means if you're a visual thinker, your system might rely heavily on color-coded files or visual maps of tasks. If you're someone who thrives on technology, digital tools and apps could be your go-to. Just make sure you don't end up with so many apps that you need an app to manage your apps—because that's when you know you've officially entered the digital Bermuda Triangle. The process starts with a keen observation of what works for you. Take a week to note down not just what tasks you need to organize but also how you approach them naturally. Do you make mental notes? Do you tend to remember better when you write things down or when you say them aloud? Just be careful with the "saying them aloud" part—if you're like me, your neighbors might think you're giving motivational speeches to your refrigerator. These observations are the raw materials from which your personalized system will be built, ensuring your organizational strategy is as uniquely effective as your quirks!

Now, let's dive into some examples of custom systems. For the visually oriented, consider a wall-mounted organizer where tasks are represented by different colored Post-it notes. This method not only gives you a clear visual representation of your tasks but also allows you to physically move tasks around as your priorities shift. For those who are more tech-savvy, setting up a digital dashboard that integrates all your calendars, to-do lists, and reminders can provide a centralized digital control center that is accessible across all your devices. This can be especially helpful if you find yourself often on the move or juggling various projects across different platforms.

Adaptation is a crucial feature of any personalized system. As your life evolves—perhaps you start a new job, move to a different city, or welcome a new family member—so too should your organizational methods. This continuous adaptation can be thought of as regular system updates, much like the ones for your smartphone. Every few months, take a step back to review your system. Is it still serving your needs effectively? Have there been lifestyle changes that require adjustments in your approach? This is where feedback loops come into play.

Or, if you're like me, the 'system update' comes with that same level of panic as when your phone decides to update itself at the worst possible time. You know, like when you're about to send an important text, and suddenly you're staring at a screen that says, 'Updating... 35 minutes remaining.' Only now, it's your life on that loading screen, and you're thinking, 'Well, I guess I'm going to wing it until this reboot finishes... eventually...'

Setting up feedback mechanisms is like having a built-in efficiency consultant. After implementing your personalized system, regularly check its effectiveness. You can do this by setting up weekly reviews to assess what's working and what isn't. Perhaps you find that your digital tools are great for work tasks but fall short of personal reminders, or maybe your color-coding system needs tweaking because you have too many overlapping categories. These feedback sessions can help you fine-tune your system, ensuring it remains as dynamic as your life.

Embracing a system that reflects your personal quirks and lifestyle not only makes the organization less of a chore but also turns it into a powerful ally in navigating the complexities of life with ADHD. I'm so proud of you for taking the initiative to create a system that truly works for you—it shows impressive self-awareness and courage. Remember, every adjustment you make, no matter how small, is a step towards a more organized and productive life that genuinely feels like your own. Keep believing in yourself; you have the strength and creativity to make this journey yours.

So many options, where do I even start?
Maybe I overdid it with the sticky notes...
Who knew pens could be so chaotic?
This is madness! Too many apps!
I think I've got it!
Planner
Who knew organization could be this fun?
Planner
Finding the perfect system might take some trial and error, but once you do, it can transform your life!

Chapter Checklist

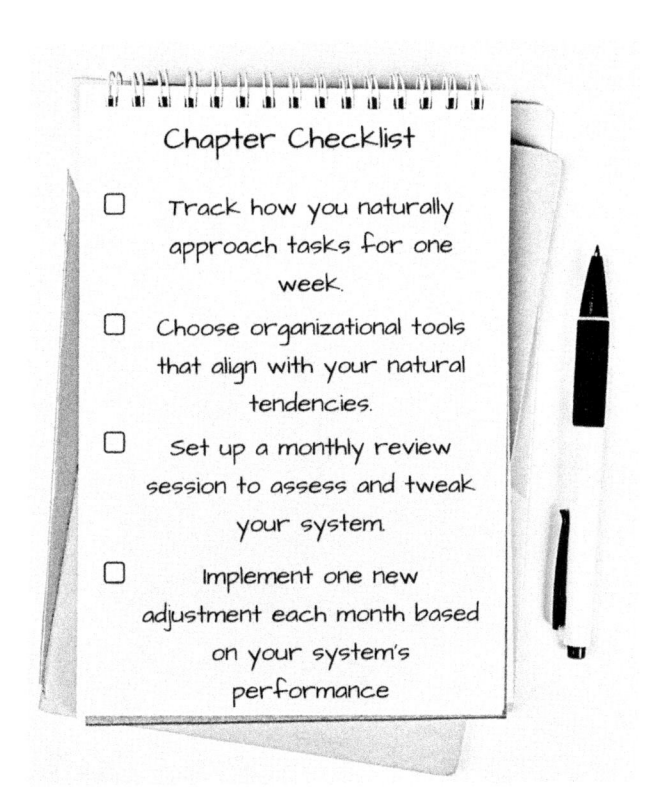

- ☐ Track how you naturally approach tasks for one week.
- ☐ Choose organizational tools that align with your natural tendencies.
- ☐ Set up a monthly review session to assess and tweak your system.
- ☐ Implement one new adjustment each month based on your system's performance

Bullet Point Summary

- Tailor your organizational system to match your personal style and ADHD challenges.
- Use visual or digital tools, depending on your preference.
- Regularly update and adapt your system to fit changes in your lifestyle.
- Set up feedback mechanisms to continually refine the efficiency of your system.

CHAPTER 1.5

SHORT SESSIONS: ORGANIZING TASKS INTO MANAGEABLE CHUNKS

Imagine trying to eat a whole watermelon in one bite. Sounds ludicrous, right? Yet, this is how many of us with ADHD often approach our tasks—attempting to conquer massive projects in a single, overwhelming gulp. It's like staring down a watermelon and thinking, "If I just give it a good, solid chew, it'll magically disappear!" But instead, we end up with sticky hands, a somehow larger-than-watermelon-sized mess, and the realization that we might need a vacation to recover. This is where the beauty of short sessions comes into play. It's like turning that daunting watermelon into bite-sized pieces, each small enough to handle easily but together making up the whole. The Pomodoro Technique, a time management method developed by Francesco Cirillo, is a fantastic starting point. Traditionally, it involves 25-minute work intervals followed by short breaks. But for those of us with ADHD, let's tweak it to 15 minutes—because the only thing worse than a watermelon is a 25-minute timer that feels like it's been set by a sadistic watchmaker. With 15-minute bursts, we can keep our nimble brains engaged without feeling like we're trying to eat the whole fruit in one go! Breaking tasks into smaller, more achievable steps is like finding the secret passages in a maze—it makes reaching the end less daunting and more doable. For instance, if you need to clean your house, don't look at it as one colossal task. Break it down: first, do the dishes, take a break, then tackle the living room, and so on. Each segment feels like a mini-victory, boosting your sense of accomplishment and boosting morale. This segmentation not only clears the fog of overwhelm but also harnesses the ADHD brain's need for frequent rewards, keeping motivation on a steady simmer.

Scheduling these short bursts of activity requires a blend of structure and flexibility. Integrating them into your daily routine can be as simple as setting specific times for these sessions—perhaps a 15-minute burst in the morning for emails, another before lunch for project work, and a quick one in the evening to plan the next day. The key is consistency without rigidity; allow yourself the flexibility to move sessions around as your day shifts. This adaptability is crucial for keeping the ADHD mind on board with the plan.

Real-life application of these techniques can transform both your personal and professional life. Let's say you're working on a big presentation for work. Instead of a marathon session that leaves you drained (and likely distracted), divide your work into multiple short sessions: one for research, another for outlining your slides, and another for adding visuals. At home, apply the same principle to manage household chores or plan meals for the week. Each task becomes a short, focused project, not a dreaded drain on your energy.

By embracing the method of short sessions, you're not just managing tasks; you're also working your energy and keeping your ADHD brain in its optimal zone of operation. I know it hasn't always been easy, but knowing you take these steps fills me with pride and admiration for you. Change is never easy, but the fact that you're here, trying, is what matters. This approach not only increases productivity but also builds a framework for sustained personal and professional growth. Each small session is a step toward mastering your tasks without becoming their servant. Keep believing in yourself—you have all the tools you need to succeed, and I'm here cheering you on every step of the way.

This is going to take forever...
Let's do this, one stack at a time!
05:00
STOP
Not now, Mr. Whiskers!
Really? Now of all times?
zzZ
Almost there!
I did it! King of the paperwork mountain!
With a bit of humor and perseverance, even the most daunting tasks can be conquered!

Chapter Checklist

- ☐ Identify three tasks you can split into shorter sessions today.
- ☐ Set specific times in your calendar for these sessions.
- ☐ Prepare a comfortable workspace free of distractions for each session.
- ☐ Evaluate your progress at the end of the day and adjust tomorrow's sessions accordingly.

Bullet Point Summary

- Break tasks into short, manageable sessions to avoid ADHD burnout.
- Use modified Pomodoro sessions (15 minutes of work) to maintain engagement.
- Integrate these sessions into daily routines for consistency.
- Apply task segmentation to both work and home projects for better manageability.

CHAPTER 1.6

THE IMPORTANCE OF ROUTINE: BUILDING CONSISTENCY IN DAILY LIFE

Let's be honest: the word "routine" might evoke visions of a monotonous, colorless life, especially for the creatively chaotic minds among us with ADHD. But what if I told you that establishing a routine is less about chaining yourself to a strict set of rules and more about setting yourself free from the daily decision fatigue that so often overwhelms us? Yes, routines can actually be liberating! They provide a framework that reduces the number of decisions we need to make about when and how to do things, which is a boon for anyone whose brain tends to run on a high-speed, scenic route rather than the straight and narrow.

Building a routine when you have ADHD can seem daunting. Still, it's entirely feasible with steps tailored to accommodate both the unpredictability of ADHD and your unique personal preferences. Start by identifying the non-negotiables in your day—those activities that must be done, like taking medication, meals, and work or school hours. Next, look at the best times for high-energy tasks versus low-energy tasks. You might be a morning person who can conquer the world (or at least your inbox) if you start before 10 AM, or perhaps your brain kicks into gear later in the day.

Once these basics are in place, begin slotting in other vital activities, like exercise, social time, and hobbies—around your energy peaks and troughs. The trick here is not to overload any part of your day and to allow buffer times for transitions between activities, which can often be a hurdle for ADHD minds that need a bit longer to switch gears. Also, consider the use of timers or alarms as gentle reminders to start or stop activities, which can help keep you on track without feeling jarring.

Maintaining flexibility within your routine is crucial because, let's face it, the only constant in life is change—especially true in the life of someone with ADHD. This flexibility might mean having a basic structure for your day but being prepared to shift things around when something unexpected pops up or when you simply aren't in the right headspace for a scheduled task. It's about having a plan but not being married to it. Think of your routine like a jazz composition—there's a melody line to follow, but improvisation is not just expected; it's encouraged. And let's be real. If my day is a jazz composition, then I'm like that one musician who's supposed to be playing the saxophone but suddenly decides to throw in a drum solo, a keytar riff, and then somehow ends up doing a kazoo cover of Beethoven. It's less 'flexible structure' and more 'let's see where the chaos leads us today!' But hey, at least I'm hitting some notes... I think.

The benefits of such a routine are manifold. Reduced decision fatigue, as mentioned, but also improved time management, better stress levels, and often, a greater sense of control over your environment and life. It's about creating predictability in a world that usually feels anything but predictable.

Take, for example, Jenna, a freelance graphic designer with ADHD who found herself missing deadlines and feeling constantly on the back foot with her projects. By establishing a routine that designated mornings for creative work, afternoons for client meetings, and evenings for admin, she not only met her deadlines more consistently but also reduced her work-related anxiety. Or consider Mark, a student who could only partially manage his study sessions. By setting specific times for studying, complete with breaks and varied subjects, he improved his retention and performance.

Embracing a routine when you have ADHD might initially seem counterintuitive. Still, with the right approach, it can become a cornerstone of a balanced, productive life. I know how hard you've been working, and I'm so proud of the progress you're making. It's not about rigidity; it's about creating a rhythm that allows you to thrive, adapting as you go, and finding consistency in the ebb and flow of daily life. Remember, you're not alone in this journey, and I'm here to support you whenever you need it. As you move through your day with this newfound structure, notice the slight shifts—less stress over what to do next, more clarity in your tasks, and maybe, just maybe, a bit more peace in your mind.

46 | EFFORTLESS ADHD ORGANIZATION

Chapter Checklist

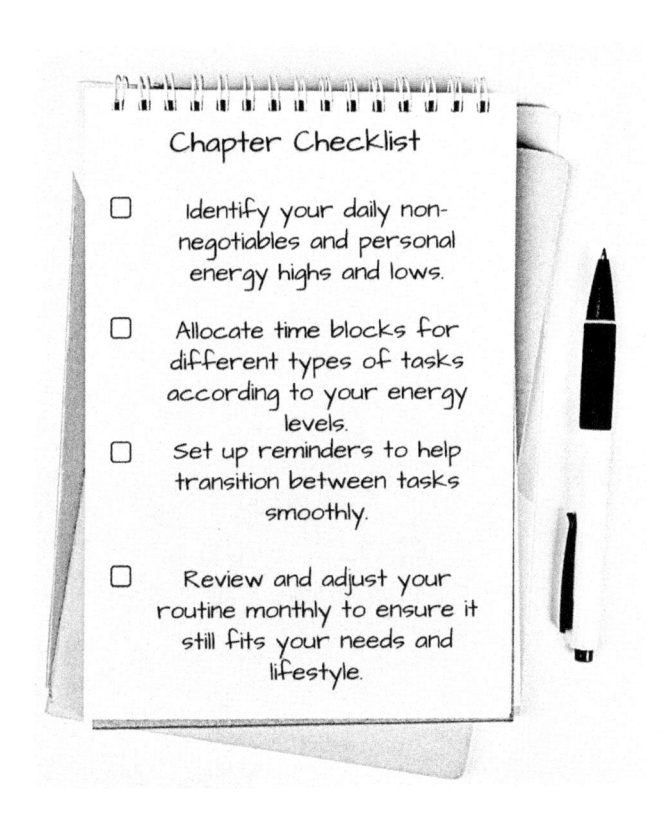

- [ ] Identify your daily non-negotiables and personal energy highs and lows.
- [ ] Allocate time blocks for different types of tasks according to your energy levels.
- [ ] Set up reminders to help transition between tasks smoothly.
- [ ] Review and adjust your routine monthly to ensure it still fits your needs and lifestyle.

Bullet Point Summary

- Routines reduce decision fatigue and improve time management.
- Tailor your routine to fit your natural energy peaks and personal commitments.
- Allow flexibility within your routine to accommodate the unpredictable nature of ADHD.
- Use tools like timers and alarms to help transition between activities.

PART II

DIGITAL DECLUTTERING AND MANAGEMENT

Ever felt like your digital life is an ever-expanding universe where emails are like comets zooming past or essential documents are black holes swallowing up your sanity? If so, welcome to the cosmic chaos of digital clutter—a familiar space for those navigating the galaxy with ADHD. But fear not as we embark on a mission to bring order to this digital cosmos, transforming it from a source of stress into a streamlined constellation of productivity and peace.

CHAPTER 2.1

IDENTIFYING AND ELIMINATING DIGITAL CLUTTER

First things first, let's define our adversary: digital clutter. It's not just those 2,000 unread emails that greet you every morning; it's also the dozens of desktop icons that have made your computer screen their permanent residence, or the multiple apps on your phone that you last opened in the last leap year. For individuals with ADHD, this clutter isn't just an eyesore; it's a series of potential rabbit holes disrupting focus and diminishing productivity, often heightening anxiety with its constant presence.

Recognizing the extent of your digital clutter is akin to a diagnostic check-up. Tools and methods for this assessment vary, from digital usage apps that track how and where you spend your time online to simple self-monitoring techniques like noting down moments when a digital mess causes frustration or delays. The goal here is to identify hotspots of digital chaos in your life—be it your endlessly pinging smartphone, your cluttered email inbox, or your chaotic cloud storage. For me, I know this process feels less like a 'diagnostic check-up' and more like finding out that I've been hoarding digital junk like a squirrel preparing for the apocalypse.

My phone alone has so many notifications; it's like the Las Vegas strip—lights flashing, bells ringing, and I'm pretty sure my email inbox is now a sentient being. It hasn't officially asked for rights yet, but I feel like we're close! The point is, don't let yourself get discouraged, and like the ADHD mascot, Dory, just keep swimming!

Once you've mapped out the territories of your digital clutter, the next step is prioritization. Not all digital clutter is created equal. Some, like those unread promotional emails, are mere annoyances, while others, like unorganized work documents, can significantly derail your productivity. Prioritize decluttering areas that have the most significant impact on your daily life. For instance, if your work requires frequent access to various documents, start by organizing your digital files before tackling less critical areas like your personal social media accounts.

The journey of decluttering is ongoing—a digital dance of sorts. Setting up a routine for regular digital cleanups can ensure that your space remains manageable over time. This might look like a weekly review of your email subscriptions or a monthly cleanup of your desktop and downloads folder. The beauty of this routine isn't just in a cleaner digital space but in the mental clarity that comes with it. It's about making your digital environment a supportive ally rather than a source of stress. When you get overwhelmed, just remember this: it's OK to struggle, and it's OK to make mistakes. We've all been there, and you got this!

Navigating through the nebula of digital clutter might seem daunting at first. Still, with the right tools and a bit of cosmic courage, you can transform your digital world from a source of stress to a streamlined space of serenity. I know it can feel overwhelming, like your inbox has become a sentient being demanding attention, but remember, it's OK to take it one step at a time.

You've already made the brave decision to address this clutter, and I'm here cheering you on every step of the way! Just like celestial navigation, where sailors use the stars to find their way, use these strategies to guide you through the digital universe, ensuring you remain on course towards a more organized, productive digital life.

This digital mess is driving me crazy!
Mails(999)
Downloads
Goodbye, random downloads!
No more cluttered screen!
Inbox zero, here I come!
Everything in its place!
Mails(0)
Digital peace at last!
Mails(0)
With a bit of humor and the right tools, even digital chaos can become a zen garden of organization!

Chapter Checklist

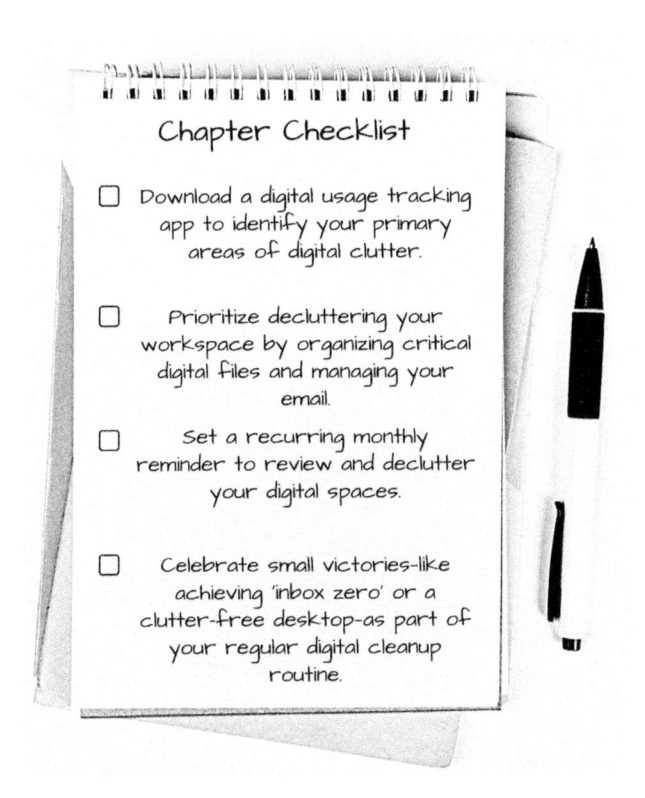

☐ Download a digital usage tracking app to identify your primary areas of digital clutter.

☐ Prioritize decluttering your workspace by organizing critical digital files and managing your email.

☐ Set a recurring monthly reminder to review and declutter your digital spaces.

☐ Celebrate small victories-like achieving 'inbox zero' or a clutter-free desktop-as part of your regular digital cleanup routine.

Bullet Point Summary

- Digital clutter includes unnecessary files, apps, and emails that disrupt focus and productivity.
- Use tools or self-assessment methods to identify where digital clutter exists in your life.
- Prioritize decluttering projects that impact your daily productivity the most.
- Establish a routine for regular digital decluttering to maintain mental clarity and order.

CHAPTER 2.2

ORGANIZING YOUR DIGITAL FILES: A STEP-BY-STEP GUIDE

In the sprawling digital landscape that is your computer, think of your files and folders as residents in a bustling city. Now, if every resident just roamed freely without any precise address, imagine the chaos! That's precisely what happens when your digital files are not organized. It's not merely about neatness; it's about making your daily digital interactions more efficient and less stressful. So, let's roll up our sleeves and turn the chaos into a well-planned metropolis.

Creating a logical and sustainable folder structure is akin to urban planning. Start with broad categories that make sense for your work and personal life. For instance, main folders like 'Work,' 'Personal,' 'Finance,' and 'Health' can act as city districts. Within these, create sub-folders to further categorize your files. Under 'Work,' you might have 'Projects,' 'Meetings,' 'Presentations,' and 'Reports.' The key here is consistency. Just as city streets are better navigated when they follow a predictable pattern, your files are easier to find when they follow a logical structure.

Now, onto naming conventions—think of them as the signs on your city streets. They guide you and save you from getting lost. Establish a straightforward, consistent method for naming your files. This might include the date, the project name, and a short description: '2020-07-15_ProjectX_Report'. Such a format not only helps in identifying the file at a glance but also keeps your files ordered chronologically. Remember, the goal is to be able to understand the content of a file without needing to open it, saving you precious time and reducing digital clutter.

The decision between archiving and deleting can feel like choosing between storing something in the attic or throwing it away. For those of us with ADHD, that attic often turns into a chaotic museum of 'might-need-this-one-day' items—like that screenshot of a funny tweet from 2012. Archiving is for files that are not needed currently but might be helpful later. These could be previous years' tax documents or past project files. Deleting, however, should be reserved for files that no longer serve any purpose and just take up space. Be decisive here—digital hoarding is as counterproductive as physical hoarding.

Utilizing cloud storage solutions can significantly enhance the accessibility and safety of your data. I know that organizing your digital world can feel like a big task. Still, I'm so proud of you for taking this step—it shows how committed you are to making things easier for yourself. Services like Google Drive, Dropbox, or OneDrive offer not just storage but also the ability to access your files from any device, anywhere. This is particularly beneficial if you collaborate with others. Remember, each small effort you make in setting up these systems brings you closer to that well-planned digital metropolis we talked about. Sharing files or folders with teammates or family becomes seamless, reducing the need for back-and-forth emails. Plus, many of these services include version history, which can be a lifesaver if you ever need to revert to an earlier version of a document. Keep going—you've got this, and I'm here cheering you on every step of the way!

Chapter Checklist

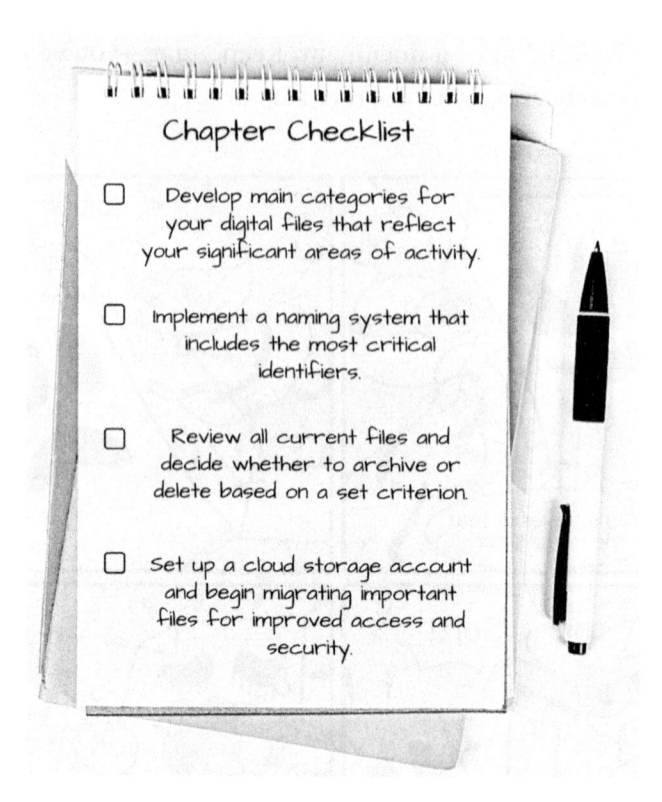

- ☐ Develop main categories for your digital files that reflect your significant areas of activity.

- ☐ Implement a naming system that includes the most critical identifiers.

- ☐ Review all current files and decide whether to archive or delete based on a set criterion.

- ☐ Set up a cloud storage account and begin migrating important files for improved access and security.

Bullet Point Summary

- Create a logical folder structure with clear main categories and sub-folders.
- Use consistent naming conventions that include dates, project names, and descriptions.
- Decide wisely between archiving and deleting files based on future relevance.
- Employ cloud storage solutions for better accessibility and collaboration.

CHAPTER 2.3

EMAIL MANAGEMENT HACKS FOR QUICK WINS

In the digital age, your email inbox can often feel like a beast that you're perpetually trying to tame. Between the newsletters you once signed up for in a moment of fleeting interest and the never-ending stream of work emails, achieving what's known as 'Inbox Zero'—a completely clear inbox—might seem as mythical as a unicorn sighting. But fear not. It's entirely achievable with the right strategies, especially tailored for those of us juggling the dynamic thought patterns of ADHD.

Inbox Zero doesn't necessarily mean having zero emails in your inbox at all times. Rather, it's about managing your email so that you're in control rather than being controlled by a constant influx of messages. It's a state where your inbox is a tool, not a burden. For someone with ADHD, the clarity that comes from this approach can significantly reduce anxiety and boost productivity. Granted, getting to Inbox Zero when you have ADHD can feel like wrestling an octopus—just when you think you've got a handle on one arm, another email pops up! The method involves regular check-ins and processing of emails to decide if they should be deleted, archived for future reference, responded to immediately, or deferred to a later date. This process reduces the mental clutter that a crowded inbox can contribute to, streamlining decision-making and prioritizing tasks more effectively.

Setting up email sorting rules is like having a personal assistant who knows exactly how you think. Most email platforms allow you to create rules that automatically move incoming emails to designated folders based on criteria you set. For example, all emails from your boss can go into a 'Priority' folder, social media notifications into a 'Read Later' folder, and newsletters into a 'News' folder. This not only declutters your primary inbox but also helps you prioritize responding to messages that are truly important, reducing the visual and mental clutter that can be so paralyzing.

The strategic use of folders and tags goes a step further in refining this system. By categorizing emails not just by sender but by project, urgency, or any other tag that suits your workflow, you enhance your ability to retrieve essential emails quickly without sifting through a pile of irrelevant ones. The key here is consistency in your tagging and folder system, which can dramatically reduce the time spent searching for past correspondence and keep your ADHD brain from getting overwhelmed by too much information at once.

To integrate this system into your life without it becoming another overwhelming task, setting a specific schedule for checking emails can be a game-changer. I know it might feel challenging at first, but I'm here to tell you that you're not alone in this—you've got all the strength you need to make this work. Instead of keeping your email open all day—which, let's be honest, for someone with ADHD is like placing a 'Distraction Central' billboard on your desktop—schedule specific times to check your email. Maybe it's once in the morning, once after lunch, and once before the end of the day—times when you're likely already transitioning between tasks. Remember, every small step you take is a victory, and I'm so proud of you for tackling this head-on! This method minimizes disruptions during your peak productivity periods and helps manage the impulse to constantly switch tasks that many with ADHD experience.

How did it get this bad?
Read Later
Yeehaw!
Abracadabra!
VIP
Take that, spam!
Promotion
FILTER
Out with the trash!
UNSUBSCRIBE
Inbox zero achieved!
With a bit of humor and the right strategies, even the wildest inbox can be tamed!

Chapter Checklist

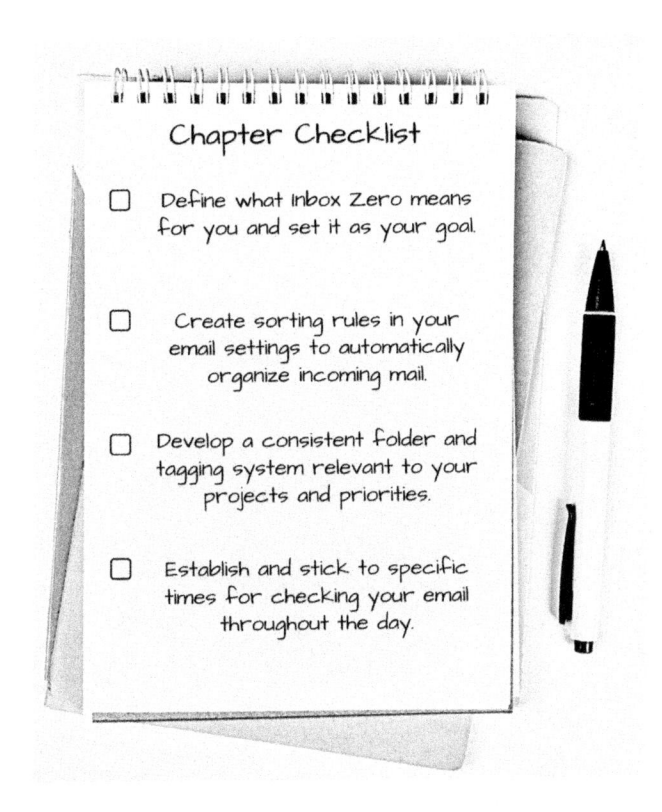

☐ Define what Inbox Zero means for you and set it as your goal.

☐ Create sorting rules in your email settings to automatically organize incoming mail.

☐ Develop a consistent folder and tagging system relevant to your projects and priorities.

☐ Establish and stick to specific times for checking your email throughout the day.

Bullet Point Summary

- Achieve Inbox Zero by regularly managing and processing emails.
- Utilize automated sorting rules to organize emails into folders based on predefined criteria.
- Employ strategic tagging and folder use to enhance quick email retrieval.
- Schedule specific times for checking emails to minimize distractions and improve focus.

CHAPTER 2.4

STREAMLINING YOUR SOCIAL MEDIA INTERACTIONS

Let's be real: scrolling through social media can sometimes feel like munching on those endless appetizers at a party—you know you should stop, but everything looks so tempting. Before you know it, you've lost an hour, or even two, just zapping through photos of your high school buddy's vacation or deep-diving into the latest celebrity gossip. For someone with ADHD, the dynamic and ever-refreshing nature of social media can be particularly entrapping, turning a quick check into a prolonged session. But what if you could audit your social media usage effectively, turning it from a time-guzzler into a well-managed activity that fits neatly into your life?

Auditing your social media usage isn't about cutting it off completely—let's face it, that's not practical or fun. Instead, it's about becoming aware of your habits. How often do you check social media? What times of day are you most active? What triggers your log-ins? Is it boredom, loneliness, anxiety, or just habit? Tools like screen time trackers can provide concrete data on your usage patterns and might just surprise you with how those 'just a few minutes' add up. By understanding your patterns, you can start to make mindful decisions about when and how you engage with social media rather than letting it be a default activity that fills up every spare moment.

Now, onto the fun part—curating your feeds. This is your digital diet. Just as you wouldn't keep food that makes you feel unwell in your fridge, it's crucial to unfollow or mute accounts that spike your anxiety, make you feel inadequate, or just don't align with your interests anymore. This curation process involves actively choosing to follow accounts that enrich your life—be it through inspiring your work, lifting your spirits, or keeping you connected to friends and family. Think of it as pruning a tree; by cutting back the dead branches, you allow healthy ones to thrive. Periodically review the accounts you follow, and ask yourself if they add value to your day or if they're just noise.

For those who juggle multiple social media accounts, perhaps for both personal use and a side hustle or job, social media management tools can be a game-changer. Tools like Hootsuite, Buffer, or Later not only allow you to schedule posts across different platforms but also enable you to monitor interactions in one centralized dashboard, saving you the hassle of logging into multiple accounts multiple times a day. These tools can help streamline the time you spend online, making your social media interactions more efficient and less scattered.

However, the key to genuinely streamlining your social media interactions lies in setting boundaries. This might mean designating specific times of day for social media checks—perhaps during a lunch break or right after work before you settle in for the evening. It also means being strict with how long you spend during each session. Setting a timer for 15 or 20 minutes can keep a quick check from turning into an unintended marathon session.

Boundaries help transform social media from a distracting black hole into a manageable and enjoyable part of your daily routine.

As you implement these strategies, you'll find that social media becomes less of a chaotic sprawl and more of a well-ordered garden where you can reap the benefits without getting lost in the weeds. I know that setting boundaries and curating your feeds can be challenging, especially when social media is so enticing. But remember, every small step you take is a victory in creating a digital space that truly nourishes you. You've got this, and I'm here cheering you on as you transform your online experience into something that uplifts and empowers you!

70 | EFFORTLESS ADHD ORGANIZATION

Chapter Checklist

- [ ] Install a screen time tracking app and review your social media usage patterns.

- [ ] Go through your following list and unfollow accounts that don't positively impact your day.

- [ ] Explore social media management tools and select one that fits your needs.

- [ ] Set specific, limited times to check social media daily, using a timer to enforce these limits.

Bullet Point Summary

- Perform an audit of your social media usage to understand your habits and triggers.
- Curate your social media feeds to ensure they add value and reduce stress.
- Utilize management tools to handle multiple accounts efficiently.
- Establish clear boundaries for when and how long you engage with social media.

CHAPTER 2.5

USING TECHNOLOGY TO AUTOMATE ORGANIZATION

Let's talk about the digital butlers of our era—automation tools. These aren't just fancy digital gadgets to show off; they are the cavalry that comes to the rescue when your ADHD brain feels like it's juggling flaming torches with one hand tied behind your back. Imagine having an assistant who remembers to send birthday greetings, schedules your appointments, and sorts your emails without you lifting a finger. That's what these tools do, and trust me, they can be game changers.

Automation tools cover a vast range of functionalities, but let's focus on those that tackle the repetitive, often forgettable tasks that clutter your mental space. Scheduling tools like Google Calendar or Microsoft Outlook can handle all your appointments, meetings, and reminders. They sync across all your devices, giving you alerts so that no matter if you're on your laptop or smartphone, you know exactly what's up next. Then there are tools like Zapier or IFTTT (If This Then That), which connect your apps and automate sequences of tasks that would typically take several steps. For example, you can set an automation to save attachments from your email directly to your Dropbox, or to post your Instagram photos automatically to Twitter.

Now, integrating these tools into your daily life might sound a bit daunting—like introducing a new member to your already chaotic digital family. However, the integration is smoother than you might think. Start small. Pick one process that eats up your time or that you frequently forget. Let's say you often forget to back up your work files. Because let's face it, with ADHD, remembering to back up files happens about as frequently as finding your glasses when they're right on your head. You could use an automation tool to schedule regular backups to a cloud service, ensuring that even on days when your ADHD has you hopping from one task to another, your backups are still being taken care of without a second thought from you.

Monitoring and adjusting your automations is crucial. It's like having a garden; you can only plant seeds and expect them to thrive by checking in and making sure they're getting what they need. Every now and then, review your automations. Are they still serving their purpose? Have your needs changed? It might be that an automation you set up months ago isn't valid anymore, or you've thought of a new task that could be automated. This ongoing process helps ensure that your digital tools evolve with you, staying as dynamic and versatile as your life.

Embracing automation in managing your ADHD is like turning down the volume in a noisy room. Suddenly, you can think clearer, focus better, and enjoy a bit more peace in your daily life. I know that incorporating new tools can feel overwhelming, but I'm here to remind you that every small step counts. You're taking control, and that's something to be proud of. These tools don't just perform tasks; they systematically enhance your ability to manage the complexities of life with ADHD, offering you not just support but a chance to excel and reclaim your time. Keep going—you've got this, and I'm cheering you on every step of the way!

Chapter Checklist

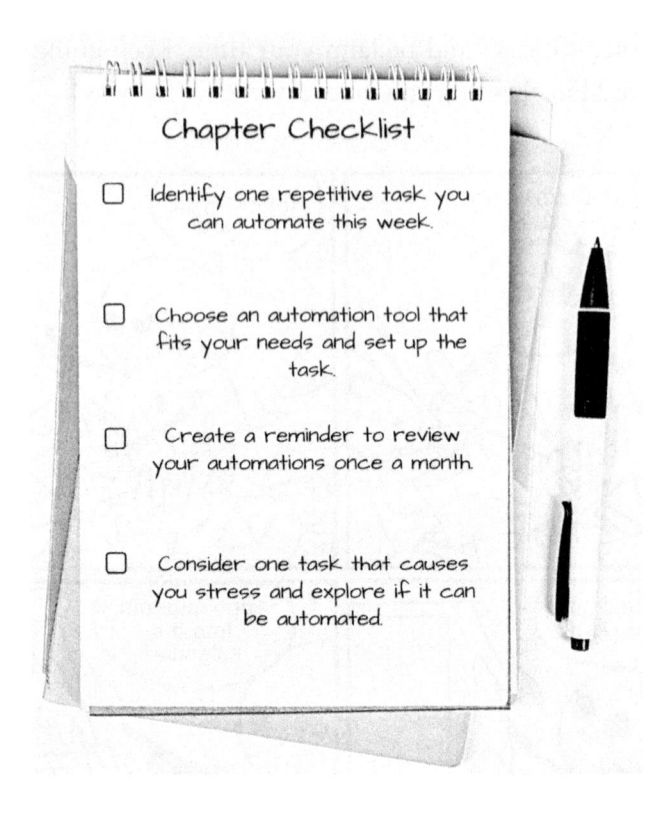

- ☐ Identify one repetitive task you can automate this week.
- ☐ Choose an automation tool that fits your needs and set up the task.
- ☐ Create a reminder to review your automations once a month.
- ☐ Consider one task that causes you stress and explore if it can be automated.

Bullet Point Summary

- Automation tools manage repetitive tasks, freeing up mental space.
- Essential tools include scheduling assistants and task automation platforms.
- Integrate by starting with automations that address your most pressing needs.
- Customize your automations to address specific challenges posed by ADHD.
- Regularly review and adjust automations to keep them practical and relevant.

CHAPTER 2.6

PROTECTING YOUR DIGITAL SPACE: TIPS AND TOOLS

In the bustling digital marketplace of your life, think of your personal information as the currency. Just as you wouldn't leave your wallet lying open on a park bench—and let's face it, with ADHD, sometimes remembering where you put your actual wallet is a win—the same level of care is crucial when it comes to securing your digital assets. Whether it's fortifying the gates against potential digital threats or ensuring that a simple mishap doesn't send your organizational efforts into oblivion, understanding and implementing robust digital security measures is a must, particularly when you're working on decluttering and organizing your digital spaces.

Let's start with the cornerstone of digital security—understanding the risks. The digital world, while brimming with opportunities, is also fraught with hazards like identity theft, data breaches, and phishing scams. For someone with ADHD, the implications are even more significant. The natural inclination towards impulsivity may lead you to click on a suspicious link or share sensitive information without the due diligence that these actions demand.

Moreover, the frequent multitasking can often leave digital doors ajar, making it easier for cyber threats to slip through. Recognizing these risks is the first step towards mitigating them, transforming your digital environment from a potential minefield into a fortified castle.

Now, let's move on to one of the most critical aspects of digital security—password management. In an ideal world, you'd have a unique, complex password for each of your accounts, as easy to remember as your own name but as hard to crack as quantum physics. Enter password managers, the knights in digital armor. Tools like LastPass, Dashlane, or 1Password can generate and store robust passwords for all your accounts, locked behind one master password. This not only eases the burden on your memory (which, let's be honest, is often already juggling a thousand things) but also significantly enhances your digital security posture. Consider this: a single, easy-to-guess password is like having one key to unlock every valuable thing you own. A password manager, on the other hand, ensures that even if one key is compromised, the rest remain safe.

Conducting regular security audits is like having a routine check-up but for your digital health. Just as you wouldn't wait for a cavity to become a root canal before visiting the dentist, you shouldn't wait for a security breach to think about digital hygiene. Setting up a regular schedule to review your security settings across your devices and online accounts can help catch vulnerabilities before they turn into threats. This might include checking for updates on your operating system, reviewing app permissions, or ensuring your firewall and antivirus settings are up to snuff. It's about being proactive rather than reactive, catching the gremlins before they wreak havoc.

Lastly, let's talk about the safety net of all digital organizing efforts —data backup strategies. If you've ever lost an important document or photo, you know the gut-wrenching feeling that follows. Regular backups act as an insurance policy against such losses. Whether it's using cloud services like Google Drive, Dropbox, or an external hard drive, ensure your data is duplicated in a secure location. Because let's face it, with ADHD, remembering to back up files manually is about as likely as remembering why you walked into a room in the first place. Automating this process can ensure it happens regularly without requiring your active involvement each time. Think of it like setting up a direct debit for a savings account—you're securing your future without having to think about it daily.

Navigating the digital realm securely requires more than just good intentions; it involves consistent, informed actions that protect not just your data but also your peace of mind. I know that taking these steps can feel overwhelming, especially when you're already managing so much. But remember, each small action you take is a victory. I'm so proud of you for prioritizing your digital safety. By adopting these strategies, you ensure that your digital organizing efforts are built on a foundation of security, making your digital space a stronghold of productivity and tranquility. You've got this, and I'm here cheering you on every step of the way!

80 | EFFORTLESS ADHD ORGANIZATION

Chapter Checklist

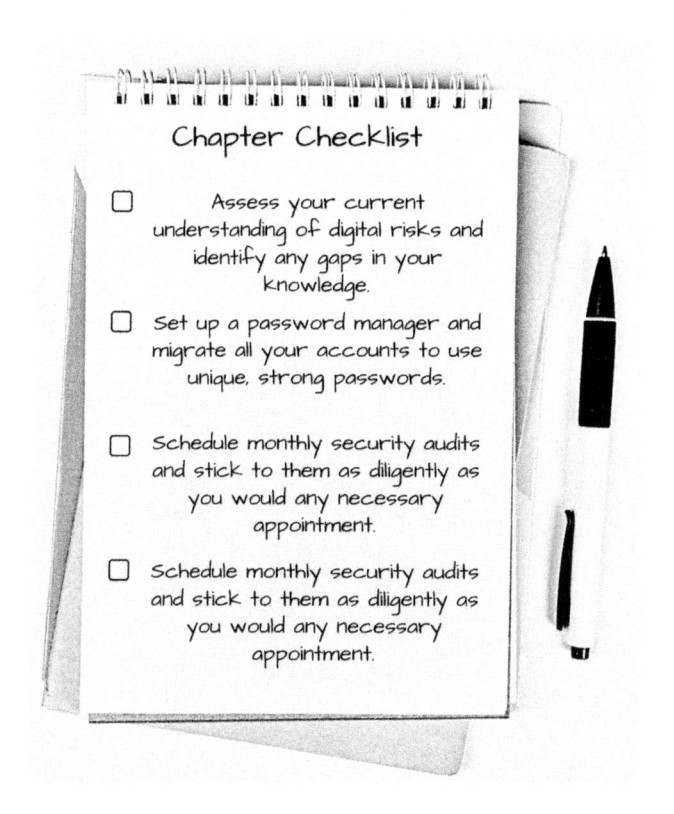

- [ ] Assess your current understanding of digital risks and identify any gaps in your knowledge.
- [ ] Set up a password manager and migrate all your accounts to use unique, strong passwords.
- [ ] Schedule monthly security audits and stick to them as diligently as you would any necessary appointment.
- [ ] Schedule monthly security audits and stick to them as diligently as you would any necessary appointment.

Bullet Point Summary

- Understand and recognize the digital security risks, especially prevalent when organizing digital spaces.
- Implement robust password management using reliable password managers to enhance security.
- Regularly conduct security audits to identify and mitigate potential vulnerabilities.
- Establish and maintain rigorous data backup strategies to safeguard against data loss.

PART III

HOME ORGANIZATION: ROOM-BY-ROOM STRATEGIES

Ever felt like your home is a live-action museum of modern chaos? Where every surface seems to magnetically attract stuff, the same way light attracts moths on a warm summer evening? If this paints a painfully familiar picture, then you're in the right place. In this chapter, we're diving deep into the heart of your living space—the kitchen. It's more than just a room; it's the command center where magic and mayhem happen in equal measure, from culinary disasters to Michelin-worthy triumphs. Let's get to transforming this central hub into a beacon of efficiency and calm.

CHAPTER 3.1

THE KITCHEN: SIMPLIFYING MEAL PREP AND STORAGE

Streamlined Storage Solutions

Imagine opening your kitchen cabinets, and instead of a cascade of mismatched containers and a jumble of lids that play hide and seek, you find a serene lineup of neatly labeled bins and clear containers. Sounds like a pipe dream? It's actually quite attainable. Streamlining your kitchen storage is about creating a system where everything has a place, and there's a place for everything. Start by decluttering—yes that means saying goodbye to the ten different salad bowls—and then introduce storage solutions that fit your kitchen's needs. Clear containers are not just aesthetically pleasing; they allow you to see what's inside without playing the guessing game. Implementing a labeling system takes the guesswork out of cooking and is especially helpful when you're in a rush and need to find ingredients quickly. Labels can be as simple as masking tape and a marker or as fancy as a label maker.

Simplifying Meal Preparation

Now, let's talk meal prep, and no, it doesn't have to be an all-day affair that leaves you feeling like you've run a culinary marathon. Simplifying meal preparation is about smart planning. Batch cooking, for instance, is a lifesaver. Imagine cooking large quantities of a base ingredient like chicken, rice, or beans and then using them in different recipes throughout the week. Suddenly, dinner is no longer a daunting task but just a quick assembly job. Thematic meal nights can also reduce the decision fatigue that often accompanies meal time. Taco Tuesdays, Stir-Fry Wednesdays, and Pizza Fridays not only make grocery shopping more manageable but also add a fun twist to dinners at home.

Organizing Pantry and Fridge

Organizing your pantry and fridge might seem like a task for the hyper-organized. Still, it's actually doable with a simple method—the FIFO (First In, First Out) technique. It's a strategy borrowed from the retail world, ensuring that older stock (or, in your case, older food items) gets used before newer ones. Start by placing newer items at the back and moving older ones to the front. This method not only keeps your food fresh but also minimizes waste, saving you money and frequent trips to the grocery store. And let's be honest, for those of us with ADHD, discovering a can of beans from 2015 at the back of the pantry is like finding a relic from a bygone era—we're just not sure if it's safe to touch! For added efficiency, group ingredients together based on type or usage. Baking items on one shelf, breakfast items on another, and so on makes finding what you need a breeze.

Tools and Gadgets to Aid Organization

In the world of kitchen gadgets, less is often more. Choose tools that multitask and save space. A high-quality food processor, for instance, can chop, dice, slice, and even knead dough, eliminating the need for multiple single-use items. Similarly, silicone lids are a great alternative to traditional pot lids and plastic wrap, as they can stretch to fit a variety of pot sizes and are perfect for covering leftovers.

Armed with these strategies, your kitchen can transform from a battleground of culinary chaos to a haven of culinary creativity. I know that starting this journey might feel a bit overwhelming, but remember, every small step you take makes a big difference. I'm so proud of you for taking charge and turning your kitchen into a space that brings you joy. Each step, from streamlined storage to simplified meal prep, is about making your kitchen work for you, not against you. As you implement these changes, notice the shift not just in your space but in your stress levels and enjoyment of cooking. Here's to conquering the kitchen chaos, one organized shelf at a time.

This kitchen needs a serious makeover!
Oops, that's not right!
SOUP
FLOUR
Unexpected refreshment!
Fashionable and functional!
Achoo! But worth it!
Mission accomplished! Everything in its place!
With a bit of humor and determination, even the messiest kitchen can become an organizer's paradise!

Chapter Checklist

☐ Declutter your kitchen by removing unused items and duplicate tools.

☐ Invest in clear storage containers and a label maker.

☐ Plan your meals for the week and prep base ingredients in advance.

☐ Rearrange your pantry and fridge using the FIFO method.

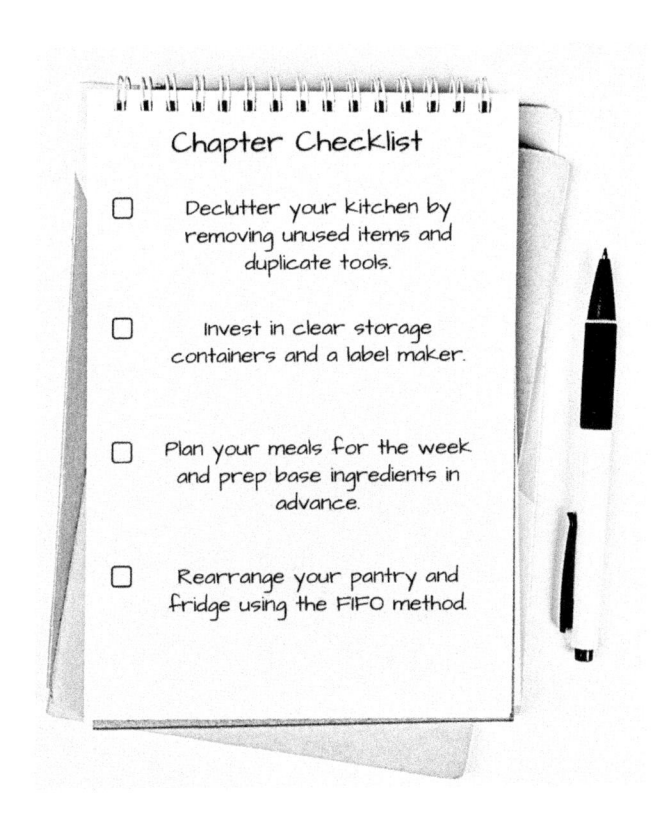

Bullet Point Summary

- Use clear containers and a consistent labeling system for easy access and identification.
- Implement batch cooking and thematic meal nights to simplify meal preparation.
- Organize your pantry and fridge with the FIFO method to minimize food waste.
- Select multitasking tools and gadgets that save space and increase efficiency.

CHAPTER 3.2

THE LIVING ROOM: MAINTAINING ORDER IN SHARED SPACES

Ah, the living room—often the heart and soul of your home, where comfort meets chaos in a ballet of daily life. It's where you collapse after a long day, entertain friends, or perhaps watch your toddlers turn couch cushions into fortresses. Keeping this multifunctional space organized is not just about aesthetics; it's about functionality and peace of mind. Let's transform this central arena from a battleground of misplaced remotes and magazine pile-ups into a serene space that serves your needs without sacrificing style.

Decluttering Common Areas

The first step in mastering the mess is embracing the art of decluttering, and yes, it truly is an art form, especially in a space that sees as much daily activity as your living room. Start by assessing what really needs to be in this space. Those magazines from two years ago? Probably not. The ten different throw pillows? Maybe choose your favorite five. This isn't just about throwing things away; it's about curating your space to reflect and accommodate your current lifestyle. Once you've slimmed down to the essentials, consider incorporating multifunctional furniture—a coffee table with storage compartments, ottomans with lids, or couches with built-in drawers. These pieces are game-changers, offering cozy aesthetics while hiding away blankets, toys, or other living room essentials.

Zone Creation for Activities

Now, think about dividing your living room into designated zones. This strategy works wonders, especially in a household with kids or multiple roommates, where everyone might be doing something different at the same time. Start by defining the activities that usually happen in your living room: entertainment, reading, playing, or maybe even a workspace. Assign specific areas for these activities. For instance, have all your reading materials near your favorite armchair to create a mini reading nook or set up a particular corner with all gaming consoles and accessories for entertainment. Of course, if you're like me, you'll set up a workspace but somehow end up napping there instead—but hey, at least the zones look organized! These zones not only help in arranging the space better but also create a mental map for everyone in the house so things are more likely to be returned to their designated spots.

Aesthetic and Functional Decorating Tips

As you streamline your space, remember that functionality should go hand in hand with aesthetics. The living room, after all, is where life happens. It's okay for it to look lived-in, but let's aim for ordered charm rather than chaotic confusion. Use colors and textures that have a calming effect—soft blues and greens, warm earth tones, or whatever hues soothe your soul. Consider clever ways to hide cables and tech devices; perhaps use a decorative box to house your chargers or a wooden panel to disguise the wires from your entertainment center. These small changes not only reduce visual clutter but also enhance the overall feel of the space, making it a place where you can truly relax and unwind.

Maintaining Shared Spaces

Lastly, maintaining order in a shared space is a team sport. It's about involving everyone who uses the space to keep it tidy and functional. Implement a simple, straightforward system of reminders or chore charts, especially if you have kids. Maybe there's a fun check-list on the fridge that assigns tasks like 'fluff the pillows' or 'stack the magazines.' And if you're anything like me, the fridge is the perfect spot—because it's the one place we never forget to check! For adults, a shared digital reminder system might work better. Acknowledge and celebrate when the space is kept well—it's about building habits together, so the responsibility doesn't fall on just one person. This communal effort not only keeps your living room in check but also fosters a sense of shared responsibility and care for the shared home environment.

By rethinking how you organize and maintain your living room, transforming it from a clutter magnet to a structured yet cozy space becomes less of a chore and more of a creative project, where every choice enhances both the beauty and the functionality of this essential space. I know starting this process might feel a bit overwhelming, but remember, every small step you take makes a big difference. You've got a remarkable eye for creating spaces that reflect who you are, and I'm so excited to see how your living room transforms. As you implement these strategies, watch as your living room turns into a haven that not only looks great but also works efficiently, making everyday living smoother and more enjoyable.

Chapter Checklist

- ☐ Evaluate and remove unnecessary items from the living room.
- ☐ Invest in at least one piece of multifunctional furniture.
- ☐ Assign specific zones for activities and arrange furniture and items accordingly.
- ☐ Set up a reminder system for decluttering and organizing that includes all family members.

Bullet Point Summary

- Declutter essential items and use multifunctional furniture for hidden storage.
- Create designated zones for different activities to maintain order.
- Decorate with calming colors and smart solutions for hiding cables.
- Involve all household members in maintaining the space with a system of reminders or tasks.

CHAPTER 3.3

THE BEDROOM: CREATING A CALM AND ORGANIZED RETREAT

Transforming your bedroom into a serene oasis might seem like a luxury reserved for those without ADHD, whose minds don't constantly buzz with unspent energy and racing thoughts. However, creating a calm and organized retreat is not just about indulgence; it's a fundamental step towards better sleep and, by extension, a more balanced life. It starts with minimizing distractions, particularly the electronic kind. Your bedroom should be a tech-free zone as much as possible. This means bidding goodnight to your smartphone, tablet, or laptop well before bedtime. The blue light emitted by screens can significantly disrupt your natural sleep patterns by inhibiting the secretion of melatonin, the hormone responsible for regulating sleep-wake cycles. Consider investing in an old-school alarm clock to replace the phone alarm you might sleep with under your pillow, or if you must keep your phone nearby for emergency calls, switch it to night mode to minimize its impact on your sleep.

Beyond electronics, your bedroom's physical clutter can also be a significant source of distraction. Work materials, exercise equipment, or even that pile of laundry you've been meaning to fold can subconsciously signal your brain that there are tasks awaiting completion, making it harder to relax fully. I mean, who knew a pile of laundry could silently judge you like that? Try to clear your bedroom of anything unrelated to rest or intimacy. This might mean finding a new home for your treadmill or setting a nightly routine to tidy up before bed, ensuring that you're not going to sleep with a visual to-do list at your bedside.

Organizing your clothing and wardrobe is another area where a little effort goes a long way. A cluttered wardrobe can make getting ready a stressful ordeal, eating into your valuable rest or personal time. Implementing a wardrobe capsule or seasonal rotations can simplify your choices and streamline your morning routine. A wardrobe capsule involves curating a limited selection of garments that mix and match effortlessly, ideally items that you love to wear and that make you feel good. Seasonal rotations, on the other hand, involve storing away clothes that are out of season and only keeping relevant items in your wardrobe. This not only frees up space but also reduces the decision fatigue that can come from sifting through sweaters in the middle of summer or swimwear in the dead of winter.

Creating a relaxing atmosphere goes beyond decluttering; it's about crafting an environment that actively promotes relaxation. The proper lighting can make a dramatic difference. Opt for warm, soft lighting fixtures that can be dimmed to mimic the setting sun, a natural cue for your body to wind down. The colors of your bedroom walls, bedding, and decorations also play a crucial role in setting a calm mood. Soft, earthy tones or cool pastels can soothe the senses and help calm an overactive mind. Incorporating elements of nature like a small indoor plant or a water feature can also enhance the tranquility of the space. Minimalistic design principles, which emphasize simplicity and space, can be particularly effective in creating a calm bedroom environment. This doesn't mean your space needs to be stark or devoid of personality, but rather that each element should contribute to a sense of peace and order.

Incorporating a routine for preparing your bedroom each night can further enhance its sanctuary-like quality. This might involve a quick tidy-up, turning down the bed, dimming the lights, and maybe even a short bedtime meditation or reading session—whatever helps signal to your brain that it's time to shift gears from daytime busyness to nighttime rest. And let's be honest, if your brain is anything like mine, it probably needs a *neon sign* saying 'sleep time' to get the message! Somewhat ironic if you think about it! These routines not only help in maintaining the physical orderliness of your space but also play a crucial role in mentally preparing you for rest, creating a ritual that eases the transition into sleep.

These steps, while simple, can profoundly transform your bedroom from just another room where you sleep to a true retreat where each night you can escape the whirlwind of daily life, recharge, and rejuvenate. I know that creating a peaceful space can feel overwhelming, especially when our minds are racing. Still, I'm so proud of you for taking this critical step toward better rest and self-care. Remember, even small changes—like tackling that silently judging pile of laundry—can make a big difference. By reducing distractions, organizing essential elements like your wardrobe, and creating a calming atmosphere, your bedroom can support not just your sleep but your overall well-being, making it easier to face each new day with energy and focus. You've got this, and I'm here cheering you on every step of the way!

100 | EFFORTLESS ADHD ORGANIZATION

Chapter Checklist

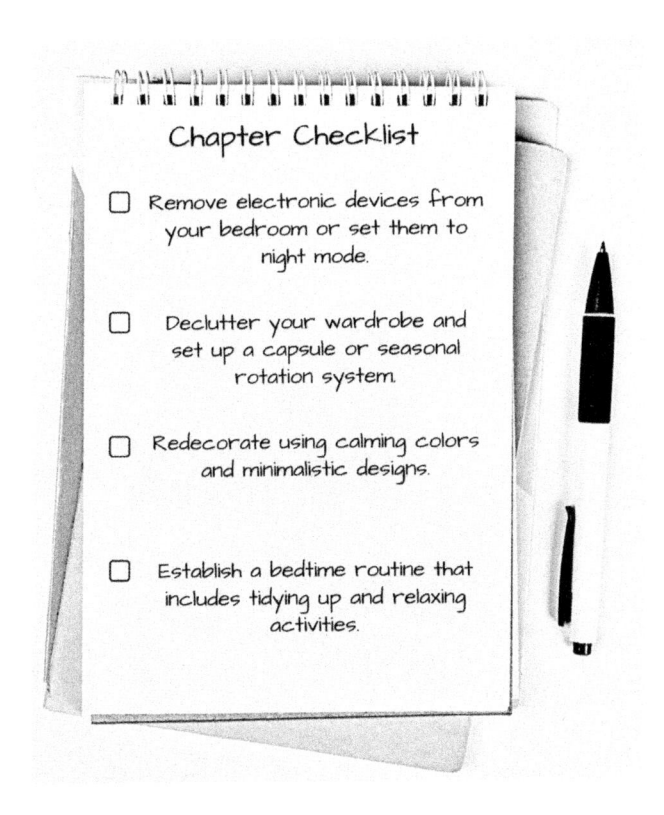

- [ ] Remove electronic devices from your bedroom or set them to night mode.

- [ ] Declutter your wardrobe and set up a capsule or seasonal rotation system.

- [ ] Redecorate using calming colors and minimalistic designs.

- [ ] Establish a bedtime routine that includes tidying up and relaxing activities.

Bullet Point Summary

- Eliminate electronic distractions and clear unrelated clutter from the bedroom.
- Organize clothing through wardrobe capsules or seasonal rotations to simplify choices.
- Use calming colors, soft lighting, and natural elements to create a relaxing atmosphere.
- Develop a nightly routine to prepare your bedroom for rest.

CHAPTER 3.4

THE BATHROOM: QUICK CLEANS AND EFFICIENT STORAGE

Imagine stepping into your bathroom on a chaotic Monday morning; you're already running late, and now you can't find the toothpaste, your favorite conditioner is empty, and let's not even start on the mystery items in your medicine cabinet. Sounds familiar? It's time to flip the script. Let's turn your bathroom from a place of frantic scavenger hunts to a zen zone where everything you need is right at your fingertips. Streamlining your bathroom products isn't just about sparking joy, a la Marie Kondo, though that's a welcome side effect. It's about functional minimalism—keeping what you need and clearing out the clutter.

Streamlining Bathroom Products

First up, decluttering. Begin with a ruthless audit of your bathroom cabinet. Yep, that means pulling everything out. Check expiration dates and toss anything that's outlived its efficacy – yes, even that sunscreen from three summers ago. It's also a perfect moment to reevaluate what 'essentials' really mean to you. Do you need five different hair serums? Probably not. Focus on keeping products that suit your daily routine and donate or responsibly dispose of the rest. This not only makes choosing what to use easier but also clears valuable space, reducing visual clutter which, let's be honest, can be a silent stress enhancer.

Efficient Storage Solutions

Now, let's talk about making the most out of every inch of your bathroom, especially if you're working with a space more 'cozy' than 'capacious.' Installing under-sink organizers is like discovering a hidden room in your house. These wonders of organization transform that awkward under-sink space into a neatly arranged haven for cleaning supplies or bulkier items. Over-the-door storage racks can be lifesavers for hanging towels, robes, or caddies that hold daily essentials. And let's not overlook the magic of transparent containers—they not only keep items contained but also let you see everything at a glance, eliminating the need to dig through a drawer of chaos for that one lip balm.

Cleaning Routines

Maintaining a clean bathroom need not be a weekend-long chore that looms over your head all week. Integrating quick, efficient cleaning routines into your daily life can keep your bathroom perpetually guest-ready without much fuss. Start with the daily swish-and-swipe; a quick scrub of the sink when you're done getting ready in the morning and a toilet brush run can work wonders. And hey, if you're like me, those 30 seconds might just be the most productive part of the day! For deeper cleans, keep a check-list of tasks and tackle one major thing each week—maybe the shower one week, the floors the next. Using natural cleaning products not only keeps the air in your bathroom fresh without harsh chemicals but also is kinder to our planet.

Accessibility and Safety

If you're sharing your bathroom with kids or someone with mobility issues, safety and accessibility should be at the top of the list. Non-slip mats are a must, and consider installing grab bars in the shower or near the toilet. Keeping everyday items within easy reach and securing medications or cleaning supplies well out of the way of curious little hands is paramount. Remember, an accessible bathroom caters to the needs of all its users, making independence and safety a priority.

In transforming your bathroom, you're not just organizing space; you're setting the stage for mornings that run smoother, evenings that are more relaxing, and a daily routine that feels less like a rush and more like a rhythm. I know taking on this project might feel overwhelming at first, but remember, every small step you take makes a big difference. You've already made the courageous decision to create a space that supports you, and that's something to be proud of. It's about creating a space that supports your life, not complicates it, ensuring that every time you step in, you feel a sense of calm and order, ready to tackle the day or unwind from it with ease.

106 | EFFORTLESS ADHD ORGANIZATION

Chapter Checklist

☐ Conduct a thorough decluttering session of your bathroom.

☐ Install an under-sink organizer and over-the-door storage solutions.

☐ Develop a daily and weekly cleaning routine incorporating natural products.

☐ Assess and enhance the safety and accessibility features in your bathroom.

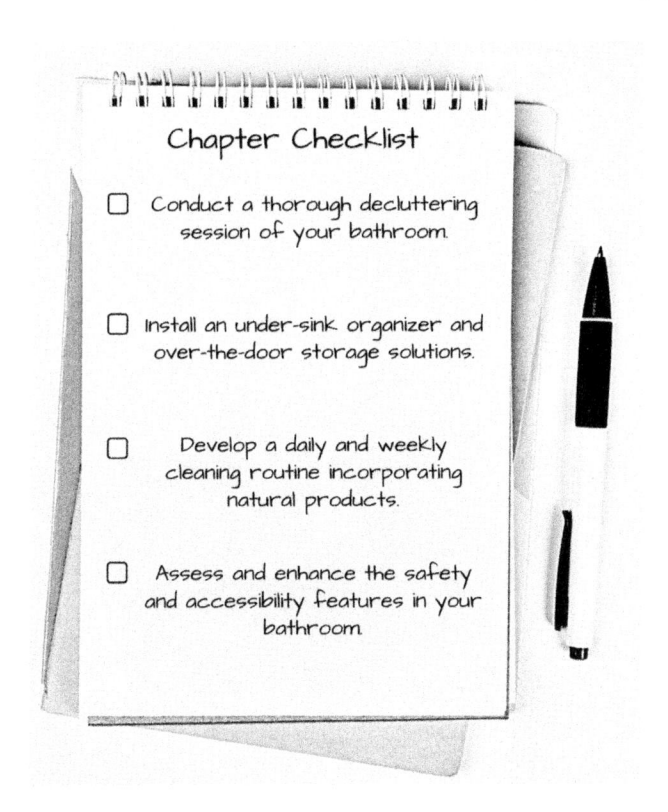

Bullet Point Summary

- Declutter and dispose of expired or unused bathroom products.
- Utilize space-saving solutions like under-sink organizers and over-the-door racks.
- Maintain cleanliness with daily mini-routines and a weekly deep-clean check-list.
- Ensure the bathroom is safe and accessible for all users, with non-slip mats and grab bars where needed.

CHAPTER 3. 5

THE HOME OFFICE: MAXIMIZING PRODUCTIVITY

Welcome to the modern-day battlefield, also known as your home office, where daily wars against distraction are fought and where productivity can either flourish or flounder. Given how much of your life revolves around this space—whether you're dialing into Zoom meetings, crunching numbers, or crafting your latest blog post—it's crucial to carve out a workspace that not only sparks creativity but also channels your inner zen. Let's roll up our sleeves and transform your home office into a powerhouse of efficiency and style.

Desk Organization Techniques

First things first: your desk, the command center. A cluttered desk often mirrors a cluttered mind, or at least, it doesn't help in decluttering your brain. For me, it's less 'command center' and more 'why are there three coffee mugs and a sock here?' Start by embracing the holy trinity of desk organization—sorting, purging, and assigning a home to what remains. Use desk organizers that appeal not just to your practical needs but also to your personal style—think vibrant colors or sleek modern designs that make you want to sit down and get to work. Cable management systems are the unsung heroes of a tidy desk. A simple tray under your desk or a clip-on organizer can turn a spaghetti junction of wires into a neat grid that would make any tech enthusiast weep with joy. And don't forget digital document management; tools like Evernote or Google Drive can drastically reduce the amount of physical paperwork you need to handle, keeping your desk surface clear for actual work.

Optimizing Office Layout

The layout of your home office can significantly impact your productivity. The placement of your desk, the type of chair you use, and even the direction you face can all play a part in how well you work. Ergonomics is not just a fancy buzzword; it's essential for ensuring you can work comfortably without risking physical strain. Position your monitor at eye level, choose a chair that supports your back, and ensure that everything you frequently use is within easy reach. If possible, set your desk up in a way that allows you to gaze out of a window. A view of nature, or even just the sky, can reduce stress and enhance creativity. Also, consider the flow of the room. Is everything positioned for easy accessibility? Can you move freely? A well-thought-out office layout not only boosts your efficiency but also makes spending time in your office more enjoyable.

Productivity Boosting Tips

Now, for turbocharging your productivity: boundaries are your best friend. This is particularly crucial in a home office where the lines between personal and professional life can blur. Establish clear boundaries, both physical and temporal. Physically, this might mean having a door you can close to signal to others (and remind yourself) that you're at work. Though, let's be honest, with ADHD, closing the door just gives you a new surface to stick Post-it notes you'll eventually ignore. Temporally, set strict office hours and stick to them as much as possible. During these hours, avoid personal tasks, and afterward, resist the urge to pop back into the office to check emails. Tools like visual timers or apps like Focus@Will can help you keep track of time and maintain productivity during work hours. Each tool should serve a clear purpose to aid your work without becoming a distraction.

Maintaining a Professional Environment

Finally, maintaining a professional environment in your home office is critical, not just for your productivity but also for how you present yourself to the world, particularly in a digital format. Invest in a good-quality webcam and microphone for those inevitable video calls. Keep the background professional and neutral; a chaotic background can be distracting and take away from the professional image you want to project. Additionally, keep professional attire handy for video calls to ensure you're always ready to switch into work mode, even if your home office is steps away from your bedroom.

With these strategies in place, your home office will no longer just be a space in your home but a launchpad for your productivity and professional success. I know that creating an organized workspace can feel overwhelming, especially when distractions are just a room away. But remember, each small step you take—from decluttering your desk to setting boundaries—makes a significant difference. I'm so proud of you for taking these steps, and I believe in your ability to create a workspace where you can truly thrive. Embrace these changes and watch as your work-from-home experience transforms, leading to enhanced efficiency, reduced stress, and perhaps most importantly, a greater sense of control over your professional life.

How do these cables get so tangled?
No more cable monsters!
Wheeee! This chair is amazing!
A place for everything, and everything in its place!
To the filing cabinet, away!
Now this is how you work in style!
With a bit of humor and the right strategies, even the messiest home office can become a haven of productivity!

Chapter Checklist

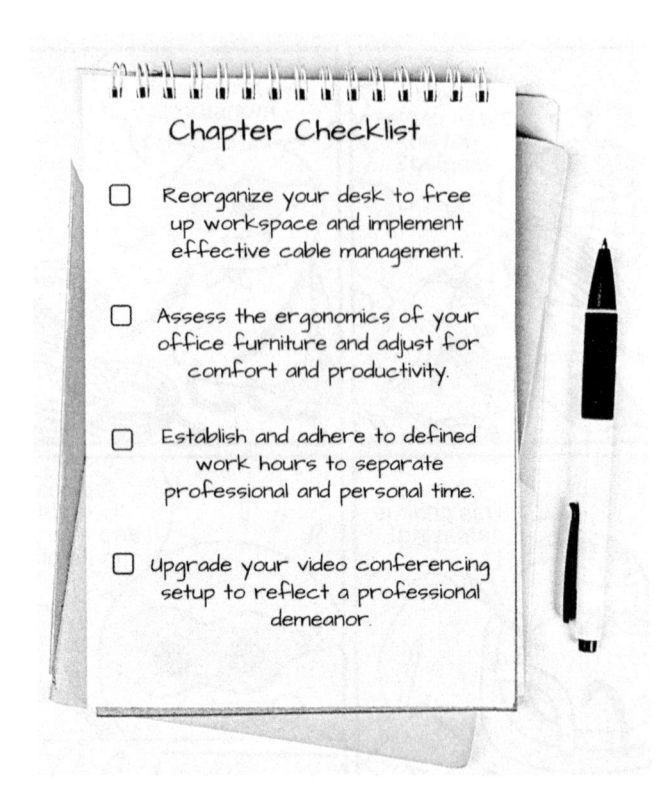

- ☐ Reorganize your desk to free up workspace and implement effective cable management.

- ☐ Assess the ergonomics of your office furniture and adjust for comfort and productivity.

- ☐ Establish and adhere to defined work hours to separate professional and personal time.

- ☐ Upgrade your video conferencing setup to reflect a professional demeanor.

Bullet Point Summary

- Utilize desk organizers and cable management systems to keep your workspace tidy.
- Arrange your office layout to enhance comfort and efficiency, with attention to ergonomics.
- Set clear boundaries to delineate work time from personal time, enhancing focus.
- Maintain a professional environment, especially for remote communications.

CHAPTER 3.6

THE GARAGE AND STORAGE AREAS: KEEPING CLUTTER AT BAY

Imagine stepping into your garage, and instead of navigating through a labyrinth of forgotten holiday decorations, sports equipment from your high school glory days, and boxes of "I might need this someday" items, you find a well-organized haven where every tool, every box, and every bike has its rightful place. Sounds like a daydream? With a few clever strategies, this can be your reality. The garage often becomes the dumping ground for all things not wanted indoors, but with the right approach, you can transform it into a functional space that serves rather than stifles.

Effective Use of Vertical Space

One of the first rules of thumb in maximizing the storage potential of your garage, or any storage area for that matter, is to think vertically. Walls and even ceilings are often under-utilized spaces that can be transformed into prime storage real estate. Installing shelves along the walls can take the bulk of your storage off the floor, making it easier to find what you need and freeing up space for more oversized items like cars or workbenches. Hooks and pegboards can be a game-changer for tools and equipment, keeping them accessible yet out of the way. And let's not forget overhead storage systems—an excellent solution for seasonal items like camping gear or holiday decorations that you don't need to access regularly. By moving these items up, you reclaim valuable floor space while keeping your belongings safe and dust-free.

Sorting and Categorizing Items

Now, let's tackle the monster task of sorting and categorizing the contents of your garage. This can seem daunting, but breaking it down into steps makes the process manageable and even satisfying. Start by pulling everything out into the open where you can see it. Yes, everything. But be prepared: you might suddenly find yourself nostalgically examining that old unicycle you bought during your 'circus performer' phase—stay focused! This might be the most challenging part, but it's essential for taking stock of what you have. Next, create categories that make sense for your lifestyle—gardening supplies, sports equipment, tools, holiday decorations, etc. As you categorize, be ruthless about what stays and what goes. If it's broken, outdated, or hasn't been used in the last year, it's probably time to say goodbye. Once you've decided what stays, invest in clear bins for smaller categories. These not only keep similar items together but also allow you to see inside at a glance, removing the need to rummage through dark boxes. Label each bin clearly and stack them on your new shelves, keeping the most frequently used items at eye level.

Seasonal Rotation Systems

Implementing a seasonal rotation system in your garage can significantly streamline how you manage space throughout the year. This system works by rotating items in and out of prime storage areas based on the season. For instance, during winter, your snow gear, holiday ornaments, and winter sports equipment would be front and center, easily accessible. In contrast, gardening tools, bicycles, and picnic gear can be stored in less accessible areas, like overhead storage. As seasons change, so does the layout of your garage. This not only optimizes your space based on seasonal needs but also prevents the year-round clutter of rarely used items. A little planning and effort during these transition times can save you a lot of frustration and time lost in searching for season-specific items.

Regular Purging Routines

Finally, establishing regular purging routines is essential to prevent the gradual accumulation of clutter that can quickly turn your organized garage back into chaos. Set a schedule for garage clean-outs—perhaps a light review each season with a more thorough purge once a year. Otherwise, you might find yourself rediscovering that collection of 'useful' cardboard tubes you swore would come in handy someday. Use these times to assess each item's necessity, condition, and whether it still serves your current life phase. Encourage all family members to participate. This not only lightens the workload but also ensures everyone has a say in what stays and what goes, making it a collective family effort to maintain a clean and organized space.

By transforming your garage and storage areas through these methods, you not only reclaim space but also bring a sense of order and efficiency to what is often one of the most overlooked areas of the home. I understand that tackling this project might feel like a daunting task, but remember, every small step you take makes a big difference. I'm so proud of you for taking on this challenge—you've got the strength and determination to see it through. This newfound organization can significantly ease the daily search-and-rescue missions that so many of us face, turning a potential stress zone into a streamlined, functional space that supports your family's lifestyle and activities.

CHAPTER 3.6 | 119

Chapter Checklist

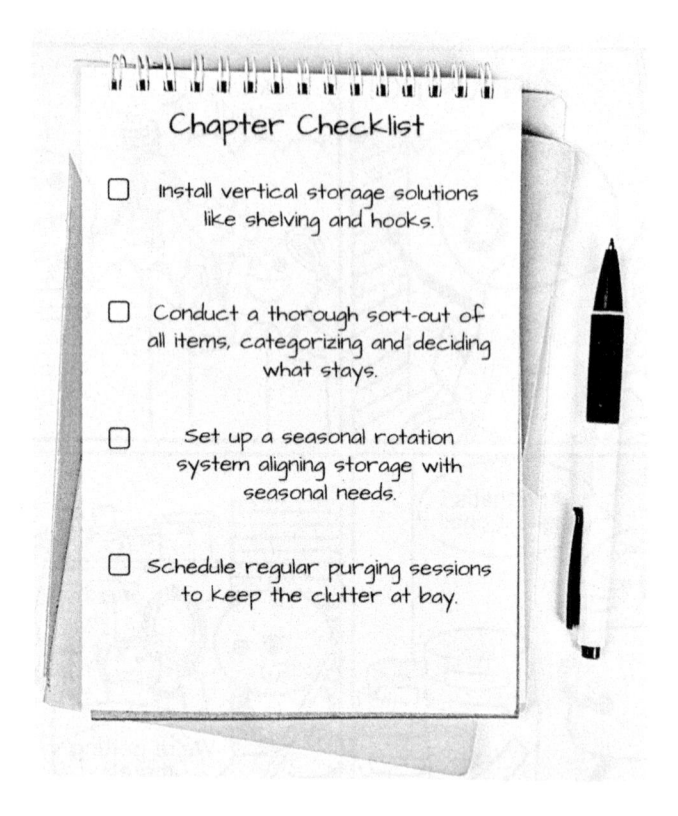

- [ ] Install vertical storage solutions like shelving and hooks.

- [ ] Conduct a thorough sort-out of all items, categorizing and deciding what stays.

- [ ] Set up a seasonal rotation system aligning storage with seasonal needs.

- [ ] Schedule regular purging sessions to keep the clutter at bay.

Bullet Point Summary

- Utilize vertical space with shelves, hooks, and overhead storage systems.
- Sort and categorize items using clear bins and labels for easy identification.
- Implement a seasonal rotation system to optimize space and accessibility.
- Establish regular purging routines to maintain organization and prevent clutter buildup.

PART IV

MANAGING TIME AND TASKS EFFICIENTLY

Imagine you're in a baking contest, but instead of knowing the exact minutes your scrumptious cupcakes need to bake, you guess. Sometimes, you pull them out too early, gooey, and underdone. Other times, they're charred remnants of what could have been a delightful treat. Welcome to the world of time blindness in ADHD —a world where time isn't just a series of ticking seconds but a slippery concept that often eludes your grasp, turning both your personal and professional lives into an unpredictable baking show.

CHAPTER 4.1

UNDERSTANDING TIME BLINDNESS IN ADHD

Time blindness isn't about forgetting the clock exists; it's about misjudging the passage of time. When you live with ADHD, time can feel like a river—sometimes flowing serenely, sometimes rushing by so fast you can barely keep up. It's like deciding to take a five-minute break, and suddenly Netflix is asking, 'Are you still watching?' This can manifest in several ways: spending hours on a task that should take minutes, underestimating the time needed for a project, or even losing track of time entirely, which can turn your daily schedule into a well-intended list of unmet goals.

The effects of this peculiar relationship with time seep into every corner of your life. Missed deadlines at work become a chorus of apologies and stress. Underestimating task durations means you're often late, whether for a crucial client meeting or a casual lunch with friends, which can strain both professional and personal relationships. At home, it might mean overestimating what you can achieve in one day, leading to a to-do list that rolls over day after day, growing like a snowball rolling downhill.

Acknowledging this time-based disorientation is your first step. It's like being in a foreign country and realizing you've been reading the map upside down. Sure, it feels like a blunder, but it's also a moment of clarity. Understanding that this isn't about carelessness or poor effort but about how your brain is wired can lift a weight off your shoulders. It shifts your perspective from self-blame to strategic management. It's about working with your ADHD, not against it.

Managing time when you have ADHD isn't about finding more hours in the day; it's about making peace with the hours you have and using them wisely. I know it can be challenging when time feels like it's slipping through your fingers, but remember, you're not alone in this journey. It's about changing your relationship with time from one of constant chase to one of harmonious coexistence. I'm so proud of you for acknowledging these challenges and taking steps to work with your ADHD, not against it. So, let's put down the baking gloves and step out of the chaotic kitchen of time mismanagement, and start aligning our clocks with our capabilities, one tick at a time.

CHAPTER 4.1 | 125

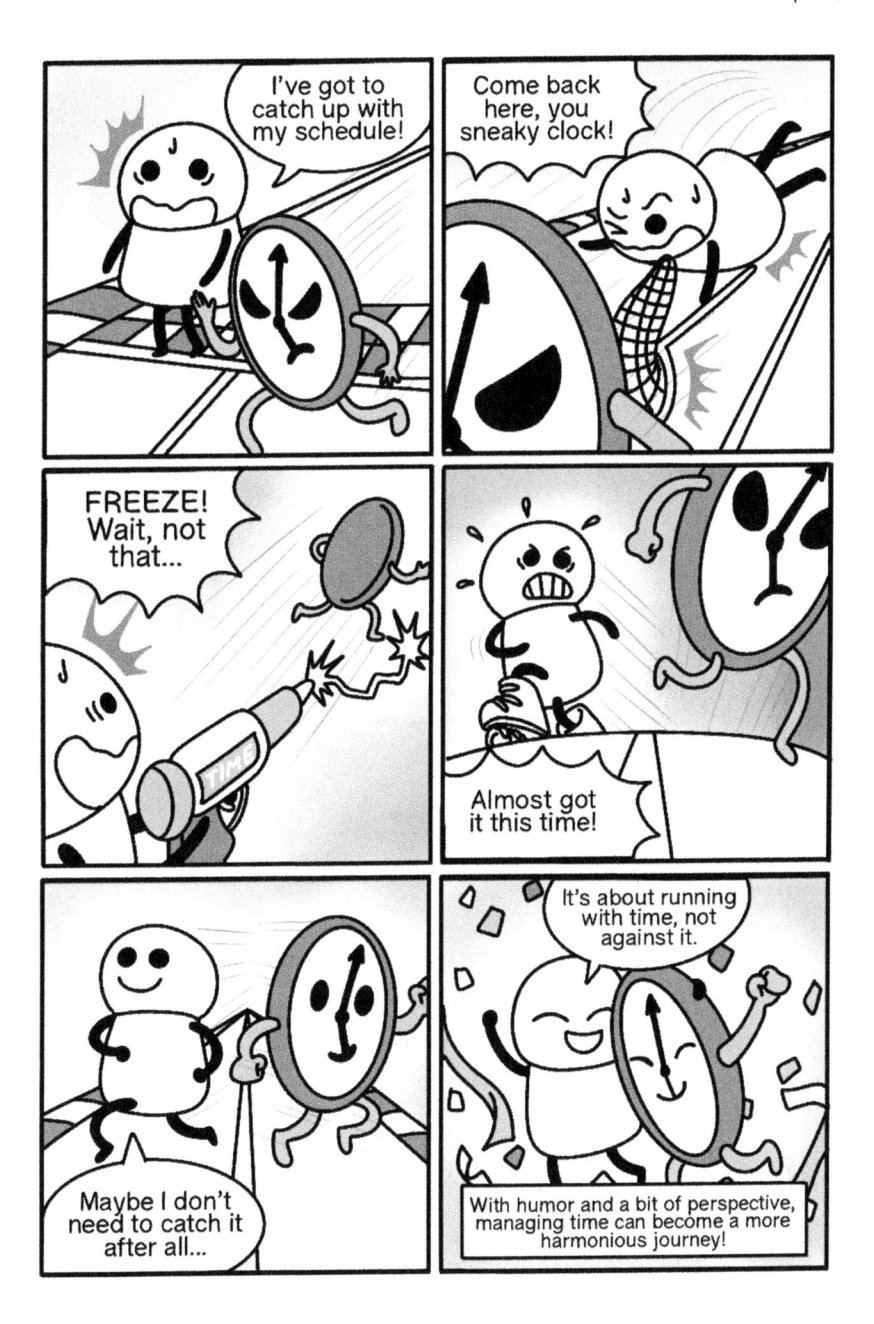

Chapter Checklist

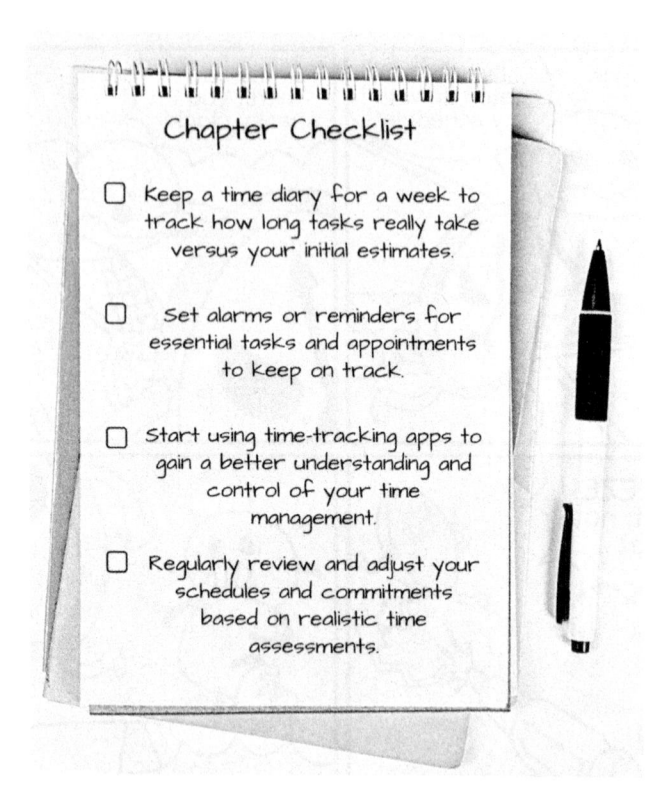

- ☐ Keep a time diary for a week to track how long tasks really take versus your initial estimates.
- ☐ Set alarms or reminders for essential tasks and appointments to keep on track.
- ☐ Start using time-tracking apps to gain a better understanding and control of your time management.
- ☐ Regularly review and adjust your schedules and commitments based on realistic time assessments.

Bullet Point Summary

- Time blindness involves a distorted perception of time, often seen in individuals with ADHD.
- It can lead to practical challenges like missed deadlines and personal strain due to tardiness or unmet promises.
- Recognizing and understanding this aspect of ADHD can significantly improve how you manage your time and expectations.

CHAPTER 4.2

TIME BLOCKING: A VISUAL METHOD FOR MANAGING DAILY TASKS

Have you ever felt like your day is a puzzle where the pieces don't quite fit? Enter the world of time blocking, a method that's not just about scheduling tasks but visualizing your day as a series of manageable, well-defined blocks. This technique can be a game-changer, especially if you're navigating the dynamic waves of ADHD. It's like turning the abstract concept of time into a colorful Lego set where everything has its place, reducing the anxiety of the unknown and helping you focus on one block at a time.

Time blocking works by allocating specific chunks of time to different activities or tasks throughout your day. It's like drawing a map of your day with precise destinations and routes. The beauty of this method lies in its simplicity and visual appeal, which can be particularly soothing for the ADHD mind. After all, who wouldn't want a GPS for their day to prevent those mental detours that end with you reorganizing your bookshelf instead of finishing that report? It helps in compartmentalizing your tasks, making them less daunting while providing a structure that can keep procrastination at bay. Additionally, by laying out your tasks visually, whether on a digital calendar or a paper planner, you can see the shape of your day at a glance—where your time is going, what your priorities are, and when you have flexibility. For someone with ADHD, this visual aspect can be crucial in maintaining focus and transitioning smoothly from one task to another.

Implementing time blocks might sound rigid, but it's quite the opposite. Start by determining the length of time that works best for your focus—maybe it's 25 minutes, or perhaps your sweet spot is 45 minutes. Experiment to find what feels right. Next, group similar tasks together to reduce the mental load of switching gears. For instance, group all your email responses together or set aside a block for all phone calls. This categorization helps in creating mental 'containers' for different types of work, making it easier to dive deep without the distraction of unrelated tasks.

Digital calendars like Google Calendar or apps like Trello and Asana can be invaluable tools for aiding in this process. They allow you to color-code your time blocks, set reminders, and even rearrange blocks if plans change, which they inevitably do. These tools act as both a map and compass in your daily journey, guiding you through your tasks while allowing for adjustments along the way.

Flexibility is key in time blocking, especially for those with ADHD. While it's great to have a plan, the unexpected is often just around the corner—a last-minute request, a longer-than-expected phone call, or an idea that catches your creative fancy. And let's be honest, for those of us with ADHD, time blocks sometimes feel more like suggestions than rules—like that 'quick five-minute break' that turns into an hour-long deep dive into the history of bubble wrap. When these happen, it's essential to adjust your blocks without feeling like you're derailing your entire day. Think of your time blocks like clay—primarily solid but malleable when needed. If a task takes longer, extend the time block and shift others accordingly. The goal is not to stick to the schedule no matter what but to use the schedule as a flexible guide that can adapt to the ebb and flow of daily life.

Embracing time blocking can transform how you view and manage your time, particularly if you have ADHD. It's about creating a visual and practical roadmap that guides you through your day, providing structure but also the flexibility to adapt as needed. I know it might seem challenging at first, but I'm here to tell you that you're not alone in this journey. You've already shown so much strength and resilience, and I'm proud of you for taking this step. By seeing your time laid out in blocks, you not only gain clarity but also a sense of control over the pace and content of your day, allowing you to focus more on what you're doing and less on what you're not.

I've got to catch up with my schedule!
Come back here, you sneaky clock!
FREEZE! Wait, not that...
TIME
Almost got it this time!
Maybe I don't need to catch it after all...
It's about running with time, not against it.
With humor and a bit of perspective, managing time can become a more harmonious journey!

Chapter Checklist

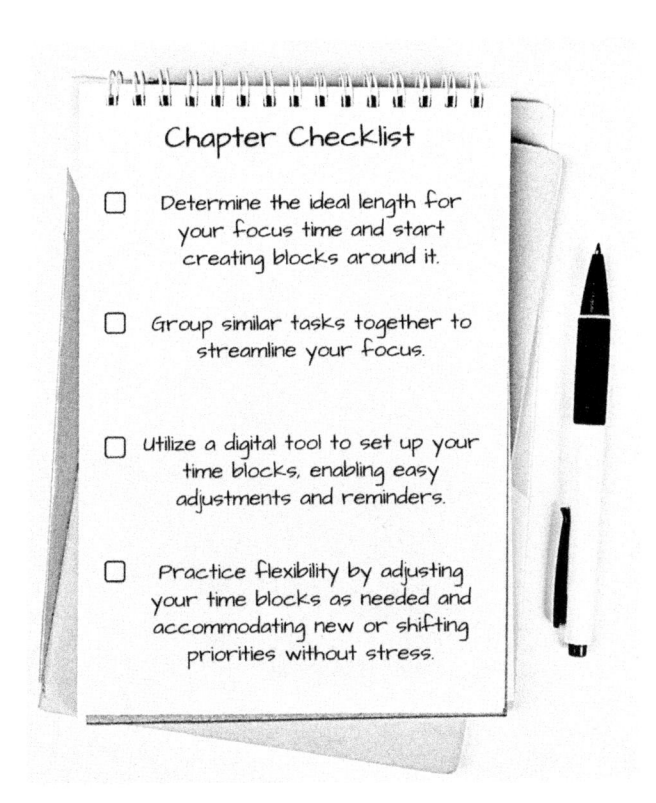

- [ ] Determine the ideal length for your focus time and start creating blocks around it.

- [ ] Group similar tasks together to streamline your focus.

- [ ] Utilize a digital tool to set up your time blocks, enabling easy adjustments and reminders.

- [ ] Practice flexibility by adjusting your time blocks as needed and accommodating new or shifting priorities without stress.

Bullet Point Summary

- Time blocking helps visualize tasks, making them manageable.
- It reduces anxiety by providing a structured way to view and tackle the day.
- Digital tools enhance time blocking by allowing for color-coding and easy adjustments.

CHAPTER 4.3

THE ART OF PRIORITIZATION: WHAT TO DO AND WHEN

Ever found yourself in the grocery store, staring blankly at the shelves, overwhelmed by whether to buy this brand of pasta or that? Or sitting at your desk, flustered by emails, tasks, and deadlines, feeling like everything's urgent? You're not alone. Prioritization can feel like a high-stakes sorting game where everything feels equally crucial. But here's a slice of relief: mastering the art of prioritization can turn that overwhelming gridlock into a manageable flow, especially when ADHD adds its own flavor of challenge to decision-making processes.

Let's break down the criteria for prioritization. Think of your tasks as applicants for the job of occupying your time. Not all applicants are equal; some align closely with your immediate goals, while others, although appealing, might not be right for today. And if you're like me, sometimes the most unqualified tasks show up with donuts and somehow get the job! Deadlines are your first filter—tasks demanding immediate attention because time is running short. Next, consider the value of each task. Ask yourself, what impact will completing this task have? Will it bring you closer to your goals, personal or professional? Finally, align tasks with your personal goals. Does the task fit into the bigger picture of what you want to achieve? This approach moves you from reactive to proactive, ensuring your energy is invested in areas that yield the most significant returns.

Tools and methods like the Eisenhower Box, or priority matrix, provide a visual framework for this decision-making process. Picture a simple box divided into four quadrants: urgent and important, not urgent but important, urgent but not important, and neither urgent nor important. This matrix helps you visually categorize your tasks and decide which to tackle first, which to schedule for later, which to delegate, and which to drop. Tailoring this to ADHD might mean adjusting what you define as 'urgent' or 'important' based on how your ADHD affects your perception of urgency and value.

Balancing daily tasks with long-term goals can feel like trying to keep plates spinning atop several poles. Daily prioritization focuses on immediate tasks—what you need to accomplish today to keep things running smoothly. Long-term prioritization, however, is about steering your ship in the right direction over time. And if you're like me, sometimes you're so busy spinning plates that you forget you're supposed to be steering the ship! Techniques to balance these include setting clear daily top three priorities while having a visible reminder of your long-term goals. Maybe it's a vision board in your workspace or a weekly review session to assess how today's tasks align with your bigger aspirations.

Now, let's talk about prioritization anxiety—the worry that you might not choose right, leading to decision fatigue. This anxiety is familiar terrain for those with ADHD, where every decision can feel weighty. To combat this, simplify your decision-making process. Limit your options—less is more. Use your priority matrix not just as a tool for sorting tasks but as a visual reassurance that you are focusing on what truly matters. Allow yourself flexibility. Sometimes, what seemed urgent in the morning might shift by afternoon. Adaptability is your secret weapon.

Mastering prioritization isn't just about getting things done; it's about making sure you're getting the right things done at the right time. It's about not just responding to life's demands but actively selecting what deserves your time and energy. I know it can be challenging when everything feels equally important, and the pressure to decide weighs heavy. But remember, you're not alone, and it's okay to take it one step at a time. With each day you apply these strategies, you'll find not only are you achieving more, but you're also building a life that genuinely reflects your values and ambitions, one well-chosen task at a time.

136 | EFFORTLESS ADHD ORGANIZATION

Chapter Checklist

☐ Each morning, list your tasks and apply the prioritization criteria to sort them.

☐ Set up your Eisenhower Box and categorize tasks into the four quadrants.

☐ Identify your top three daily tasks and review their alignment with your long-term goals.

☐ Practice flexibility by reassessing and adjusting your priorities at the end of the day.

Bullet Point Summary

- Use deadlines, task value, and alignment with personal goals as criteria for prioritization.
- Employ tools like the Eisenhower Box to visually manage and categorize tasks.
- Differentiate between daily tasks and long-term goals to maintain focus and direction.
- Address prioritization anxiety by simplifying choices and embracing flexibility.

CHAPTER 4.4

OVERCOMING OVERWHELM: TECHNIQUES TO BREAK DOWN LARGE PROJECTS

Ever stared at a mountain of tasks so daunting that you considered just curling up and becoming part of the furniture? If so, you've met Overwhelm, the not-so-gentle giant of project management, incredibly familiar to those navigating life with ADHD. Overwhelm doesn't have to be the villain of your story, though. With the right strategies, breaking down the Goliath of a project into stone-slinging Davids can not only be achievable but downright satisfying.

Let's dive into the art of decomposing those gigantic undertakings into bite-sized pieces. The key here is not to see the project as one colossal entity but as a series of small, interconnected tasks. Lists can be your first line of defense—simple yet powerful. Start by jotting down every single task involved, no matter how small. This could be as minute as sending an email or as significant as writing a report. Next, consider organizing these tasks into a flowchart. This visual representation can help you see the dependencies between tasks, allowing you to prioritize effectively and sequence tasks in a logical flow. Digital tools like Asana or Trello can supercharge this process, providing platforms where tasks can not only be listed but also moved around interactively as priorities shift.

Recognizing the signs of overwhelm is crucial. It might sneak up as a feeling of dread every time you think about the project or physical tension--a tightness in your shoulders or a knot in your stomach whenever you sit down to work. When these feelings bubble up, it's your cue to step back. I mean, if your brain starts feeling like a web browser with 37 tabs open and you can't figure out where the music is coming from, it's time for a break. Implement structured breaks to regain your perspective. These aren't just pauses; they're lifelines. During these breaks, do something utterly unrelated to the project—walk, meditate, doodle, or even engage in a quick workout. The aim is to reset your mental state, giving you a clearer, calmer approach when you return.

Incorporating buffer times between tasks can also be a game-changer, particularly for those with ADHD. These buffers act as cushions, giving you leeway if a task takes longer than expected or if an unexpected complication pops up. This practice acknowledges the fluidity of your working rhythm and respects your need for flexibility, reducing the pressure to perform with machine-like precision.

Celebrating milestones within your project is about giving credit where it's due—to yourself. Every task completed from your list or every node passed in your flowchart is a victory. And let's be honest, finishing a task without getting sidetracked by that fascinating documentary on underwater basket weaving is practically a superhero feat! Mark these accomplishments. Maybe it's a check on a physical list, a celebratory post on your project management tool, or a small reward like your favorite coffee. These celebrations act as positive reinforcements, not just cheering you on but also bolstering your motivation to keep pushing forward.

By adopting these strategies, you transform the process of tackling large projects from a battle against a behemoth to a series of victorious skirmishes. I know it can be challenging when tasks feel overwhelming, but I'm so proud of you for breaking them down into manageable pieces. Each step planned, and each milestone celebrated paves the way not just to the completion of the project but to a journey where you are in control, steering the ship with confidence and resilience, ready to take on the next big challenge with gusto. Remember, every small victory is a testament to your strength and determination, and I'm here cheering you on every step of the way.

How am I ever going to tackle this?
One step at a time!
Reports
Meeting
Emails
Let's organize these tasks!
1
2
3
4
To-do
5
Calendar
Management
Digital tools make this easier!
DONE
DONE
Almost there!
I did it!
With a bit of humor and the right tools, even the biggest tasks can be broken down into manageable steps!

Chapter Checklist

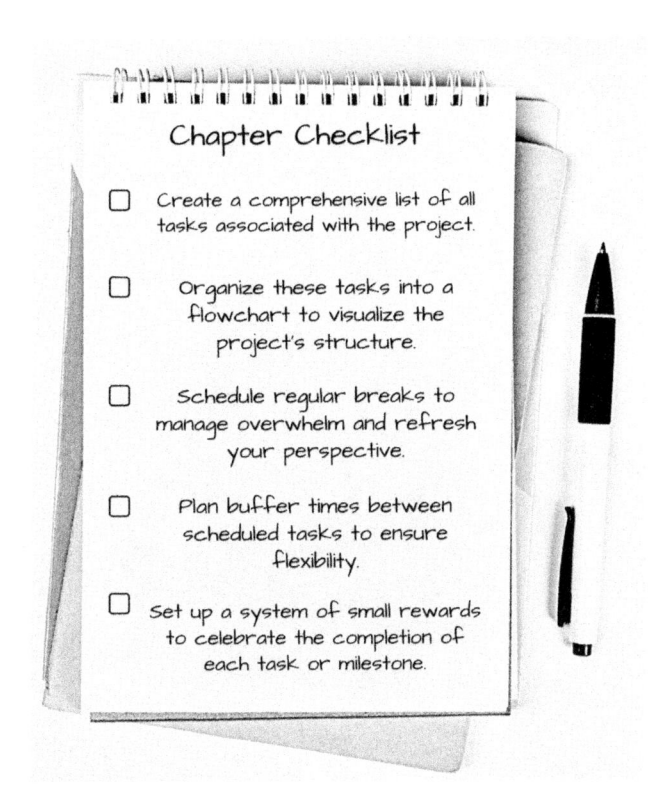

☐ Create a comprehensive list of all tasks associated with the project.

☐ Organize these tasks into a flowchart to visualize the project's structure.

☐ Schedule regular breaks to manage overwhelm and refresh your perspective.

☐ Plan buffer times between scheduled tasks to ensure flexibility.

☐ Set up a system of small rewards to celebrate the completion of each task or milestone.

Bullet Point Summary

- Break large projects into a detailed list of small tasks.
- Use flowcharts or digital project management tools to organize and prioritize tasks visually.
- Recognize and manage feelings of overwhelm with structured breaks.
- Incorporate buffer times to accommodate unforeseen delays or extensions in task durations.
- Celebrate each completed task or milestone to maintain motivation and acknowledge progress.

CHAPTER 4.5

THE POMODORO TECHNIQUE: TAILORED FOR ADHD

Have you ever felt like managing your day is akin to herding cats? If so, the Pomodoro Technique might just be the shepherd's whistle you need. Initially developed by Francesco Cirillo in the late 1980s, this time management method is not just about chopping your workday into strict slices of time; it's about creating a rhythm that can help bring order to the often chaotic ADHD mind. And let's face it, focusing for 25 minutes straight can feel like climbing Mount Everest without oxygen! The basic principle involves dividing your work into intervals, traditionally 25 minutes in length, separated by shorter breaks. These intervals are known colloquially as "Pomodoros," named after the tomato-shaped kitchen timer Cirillo used as a university student.

Now, while the traditional Pomodoro Technique has its perks, anyone with ADHD knows that one size does not fit all. Customizing these intervals to better suit your unique mental rhythms can make a significant difference. Perhaps the standard 25 minutes is too long for you, leading to waning attention and productivity. Experimenting with shorter intervals, say 15 or even

10 minutes, might keep you more consistently engaged. During these bursts of focused activity, the brain knowing there's an imminent break can help maintain concentration and reduce the cognitive fatigue that often accompanies more extended periods of focus.

Integrating adequate breaks is crucial in this adapted Pomodoro Technique. Breaks aren't merely pauses; they're opportunities to reset and refresh your mind. For someone with ADHD, these intervals can serve as critical moments to prevent mental saturation. Engage in activities utterly unrelated to work during these breaks—stand up and stretch, do a quick physical chore, or practice a few minutes of mindfulness. These activities can help clear your mental workspace and lower the chances of ADHD-related burnout.

Keeping track of your progress is another cornerstone of effectively using the Pomodoro Technique. This isn't just about ticking off tasks on your to-do list; it's about visually and tangibly measuring your productivity. Tools like physical timers can be immensely helpful—or they serve as that friendly reminder that we're supposed to be working and not suddenly reorganizing the spice rack. You can also use apps designed for the Pomodoro Technique that allow you to customize the length of intervals and breaks. These tools often come with features that let you note down what task you'll be tackling in each interval, offering a clear roadmap of your day. Seeing your tasks laid out and your progress marked in real-time can provide a motivational boost and a sense of accomplishment.

In embracing the Pomodoro Technique with these adaptations, you're not just adopting a time management strategy. You're also committing to a structured yet flexible way to enhance your productivity. I know it hasn't always been easy, but I'm so proud of you for finding methods that align with your unique rhythm. Remember, every small step you take is a victory worth celebrating. This method respects the unique challenges and strengths of the ADHD brain, offering a practical approach to managing time and tasks with a rhythmic flair that can turn even the most daunting workdays into a series of achievable victories.

148 | EFFORTLESS ADHD ORGANIZATION

Chapter Checklist

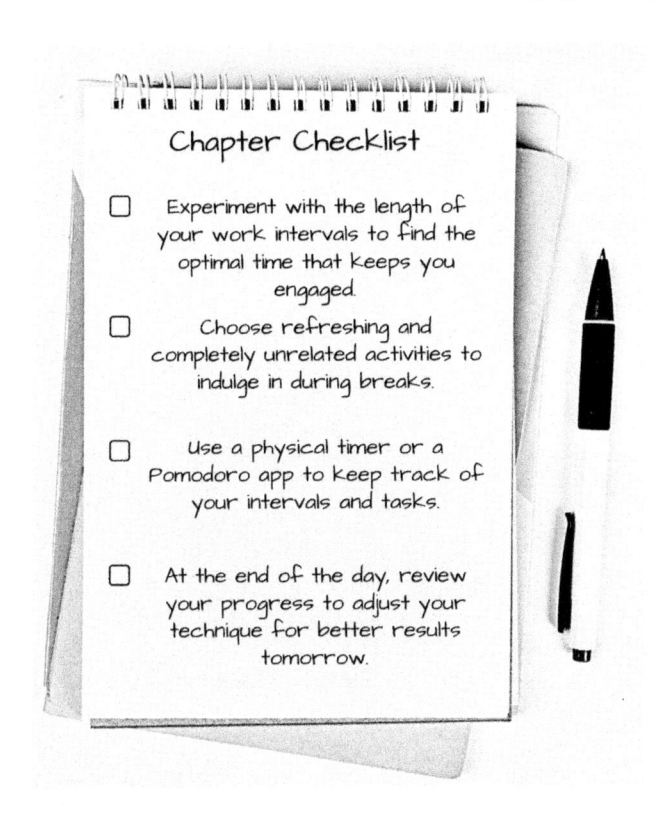

- ☐ Experiment with the length of your work intervals to find the optimal time that keeps you engaged.
- ☐ Choose refreshing and completely unrelated activities to indulge in during breaks.
- ☐ Use a physical timer or a Pomodoro app to keep track of your intervals and tasks.
- ☐ At the end of the day, review your progress to adjust your technique for better results tomorrow.

Bullet Point Summary

- The Pomodoro Technique involves focused intervals of work followed by short breaks.
- Tailoring the length of these intervals can enhance focus and productivity for individuals with ADHD.
- Breaks should be used to engage in non-work-related activities to refresh the mind.
- Tracking progress with timers or specialized apps can increase motivation and satisfaction from completed tasks.

CHAPTER 4.6

SETTING REALISTIC GOALS AND CELEBRATING SMALL VICTORIES

Ever found yourself setting sky-high goals like, "This week, I'll organize every single inch of my house, start a new diet, and maybe learn Mandarin," only to end up binge-watching a whole series while the gym card collects dust? If that rings a bell, welcome to the club! Setting goals when you have ADHD can sometimes feel like aiming a dart in the dark. What you need are realistic goals—targets that challenge you but are still within the range of your capabilities and resources.

Defining realistic goals starts with a good old reality check. It's about understanding and accepting your limits—not as shortcomings but as the contours within which you can paint your masterpiece. Consider your energy levels, your commitments, and yes, the way ADHD plays into your daily life. For instance, if focusing for long periods is your Achilles' heel, a goal to write a novel in a month might be setting the bar a bit too high. Instead, how about starting with a goal to write a page a day? It's manageable and less daunting, making it more likely you'll stick to it and less likely you'll end up feeling defeated.

The importance of celebrating small wins along this journey cannot be overstated. Each small victory is a stepping stone towards bigger successes. Did you manage to sort through your emails today? That's a win. Cooked a meal instead of ordering in? Another win. These victories, as tiny as they might seem, pack a powerful psychological punch. They boost your morale, enhance your motivation, and fuel you to keep going. Remember, ADHD can often make it hard to see the big picture when the frame is crowded with distractions. Focusing on these small wins keeps your spirits up and your eyes on the prize.

Now, let's move on to the strategies for regular review and adjustment. Setting goals isn't a one-and-done deal; it's an ongoing process that requires tweaking and fine-tuning. Regular check-ins on your progress help you stay aligned with your objectives and make necessary adjustments. Maybe you've set a goal to declutter your workspace, but halfway through the week, you find it's too ambitious given your current workload. That's okay! Adjust it. It's like realizing the 'clean desk policy' works better as a 'clear a path so you can see the desk policy.' Maybe break it down into smaller parts or extend your timeline. The key is to remain flexible and responsive to your needs, not rigidly adherent to a plan that's no longer serving you.

Using visual aids for goal tracking can be especially effective if you're a visual learner or someone who finds satisfaction in seeing progress tangibly. Charts, progress bars, or even a simple checklist on a whiteboard can offer daily reminders of what you're aiming for and how far you've come. They serve as both a prompt and a reward, visually mapping out your journey and giving you that little dopamine hit every time you get to draw a line through a completed task.

Incorporating these strategies into your goal-setting routine transforms the process from a daunting chore into an engaging, rewarding journey. I know it can be tricky when your enthusiasm wants to conquer everything at once, but remember that every outstanding achievement starts with a single step. I'm so proud of you for recognizing the importance of setting realistic goals and celebrating those small victories along the way. Keep believing in yourself—you've got the strength and determination to turn your aspirations into reality. It's about knowing when to push and when to pivot, celebrating the steps along the way, and visually charting your progress to keep the destination clear. So, grab those markers, start plotting your course, and let each small victory bring a splash of color to the canvas of your achievements.

154 | EFFORTLESS ADHD ORGANIZATION

Chapter Checklist

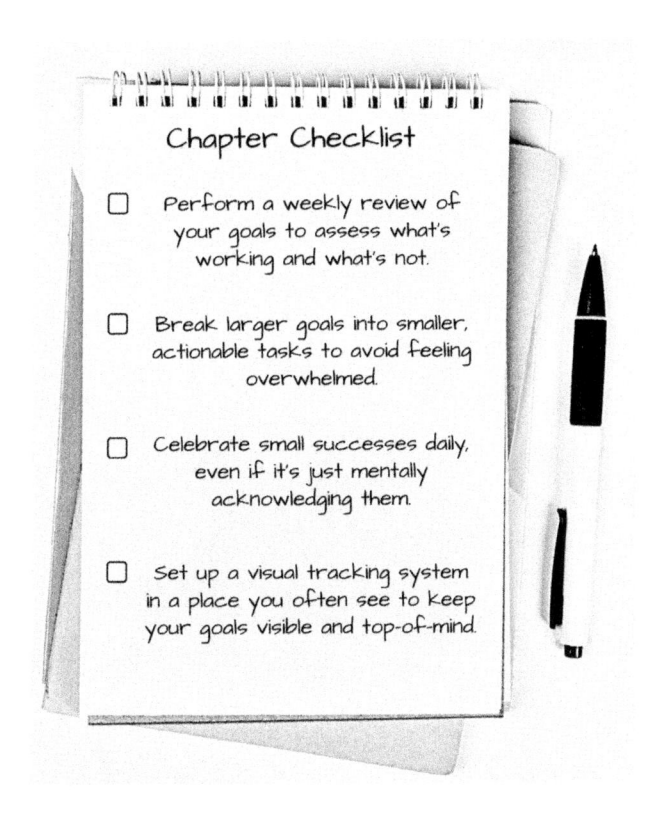

☐ Perform a weekly review of your goals to assess what's working and what's not.

☐ Break larger goals into smaller, actionable tasks to avoid feeling overwhelmed.

☐ Celebrate small successes daily, even if it's just mentally acknowledging them.

☐ Set up a visual tracking system in a place you often see to keep your goals visible and top-of-mind.

Bullet Point Summary

- Set achievable goals that consider your energy, commitments, and ADHD traits.
- Celebrate every small victory to boost morale and motivation.
- Regularly review and adjust your goals to ensure they remain realistic and aligned with your circumstances.
- Use visual aids like charts or progress bars to track and motivate progress on your goals.

CHAPTER 4.7

AVOIDING COMMON TIME MANAGEMENT PITFALLS

Let's face it, even the best-laid plans can scatter like a deck of cards in a breeze, especially when ADHD is in the mix. It's like setting your GPS for a smooth ride home, only to find every turn leads to unexpected detours and delays. Understanding these time management pitfalls is like having a road map of potential potholes so you can steer clear rather than fall in. Common pitfalls for those with ADHD include underestimating how much time tasks truly require or the classic trap of multitasking, where spreading your focus too thin ends up spreading you too thin as well.

What if we approached these pitfalls not as roadblocks but as bends in the road, requiring a bit of careful navigation? For instance, the chronic underestimation of time needed for tasks isn't just about poor guessing; it's often a misjudgment of what the task entails or a hopeful optimism about our efficiency. I mean, who hasn't thought, 'I'll just clean the whole house in 30 minutes,' and then three hours later, you're deep cleaning the toaster. Start by becoming a student of your own habits. Track how long each task actually takes versus how long you thought it would take. This isn't about self-reproof but about gathering data to better inform your future estimates. Tools like Toggl or RescueTime can automate this tracking, offering insights without requiring much effort from you.

Now, let's talk multitasking—often a go-to method for those with ADHD, driven by a restless mind hungry for stimulation. Yet, this can lead to a cycle of starting much but finishing little. The antidote? Embrace single-tasking. This means committing to one task at a time, giving it your full attention until it's complete or reaches a natural stopping point. It sounds simple, but it's a profound shift from how many ADHD minds operate. To aid this, use physical cues to define your focus area—perhaps a dedicated workspace for each type of task, or a specific notebook or digital device that's only used for one project.

Learning from mistakes in time management isn't just good practice; it's essential. Every missed deadline or over-run project is ripe with lessons. Adopt a mindset that views these not as failures, but as feedback. I mean, sure, missing a deadline feels like the end of the world, but hey, at least it's a great time to reflect—preferably while stress-eating snacks you forgot you bought. Regularly review what went awry and why. Was it poor planning? Was the project scope too large? Did unexpected tasks throw you off course? This reflection turns mistakes into stepping stones towards more robust time management strategies.

Preventative measures can safeguard against future time management mishaps. Regular planning sessions, for instance, can help you stay ahead of your schedule rather than racing behind it. Consider weekly planning sessions where you map out your goals, tasks, and appointments for the week ahead. Use this time to set up reminder systems, too—digital alerts, sticky notes, or daily check-ins with a partner or coach can keep you on track. The goal here is to create a safety net of reminders and checks that keep you moving forward, even when your focus might waver.

Navigating the world of time management with ADHD doesn't have to feel like a constant uphill battle. I understand how challenging it can be, but I want you to know that you're making incredible strides every day. The fact that you're here, looking for ways to improve, already shows your commitment to progress. With the right strategies, a bit of self-awareness, and tools that leverage your strengths, you can transform potential pitfalls into landscapes of productivity. Remember, every time you learn from a misstep or embrace a new approach, you're turning obstacles into opportunities. It's about setting up systems that compensate for the quirks of ADHD, allowing you to manage time as effectively as anyone else, if not better. You've got this, and I'm here cheering you on every step of the way!

160 | EFFORTLESS ADHD ORGANIZATION

Chapter Checklist

- ☐ Begin tracking time spent on tasks for one week to identify estimation errors.
- ☐ Choose one project daily to apply single-tasking and note the differences in outcome.
- ☐ Reflect weekly on any time management challenges and what you can learn from them.
- ☐ Set up a weekly planning session to organize and prepare for upcoming tasks.
- ☐ Implement a reminder system that works for you-digital alerts, desk notes, or accountability check-ins.

Bullet Point Summary

- Common pitfalls include underestimating task duration and excessive multitasking.
- Track actual time spent on tasks to improve estimation accuracy.
- Focus on single-tasking to enhance completion rates.
- Learn from past time management mistakes to refine strategies.
- Implement regular planning and reminder systems to prevent future pitfalls.

PART V

ADHD AND FAMILY LIFE

Picture this: You're planning a family outing. Sounds simple, right? But then the ADHD kicks in, and suddenly you're trying to herd cats in a tornado. Everyone's interests are swirling around; no one can decide where to go or what to do, and you're just standing there, wishing you had a magic wand to make it all come together smoothly. Well, let's roll up our sleeves and conjure up that magic with some practical, ADHD-friendly strategies to organize family activities without the usual chaos.

CHAPTER 5.1

ORGANIZING FAMILY ACTIVITIES WITH EASE

Organizing family activities can feel a bit like trying to solve a Rubik's cube blindfolded. But what if I told you there are tools and systems designed to make this not only manageable but actually enjoyable? Let's dive into some strategies that can turn planning from a stress-inducing ordeal into an easy, breezy process, even with ADHD in the mix.

Activity Planning Systems

First up, let's talk about the digital wizards of organization: shared digital calendars and family planning apps. These aren't just tools; they're your allies. Apps like Cozi or Google Family Calendar allow you to synchronize activities across everyone's devices. Imagine this: no more double bookings or missed soccer games because everyone knows who needs to be where and when. It's like having a family command center at your fingertips. These tools often offer features tailored for ADHD needs, like setting multiple reminders for upcoming events—because sometimes one just isn't enough—and color-coding activities by family member, which can help in visually distinguishing between everyone's schedules at a glance.

Simplifying Activity Choices

Now, on to decision-making, which can be a battlefield for ADHD minds, with too many options leading to decision paralysis. Simplifying choices can be your strategy for victory. And let's be honest when faced with too many choices, I've spent more time deciding what to have for dinner than it took to actually cook it. Setting themes for days or activities can narrow down the overwhelming array of options. Think 'Water Wednesdays' for anything from visiting a local pool to running through sprinklers in the backyard, or 'Foodie Fridays' where the family tries a new restaurant or cooks a new recipe together. This not only makes deciding easier but also adds a fun twist to regular activities, keeping engagement high and stress low.

Preparation Check-lists

Preparation is key, especially when ADHD is in the picture. Last-minute rushes can amplify stress and lead to forgotten essentials—like leaving the picnic basket next to the door and realizing it halfway to the park. Check-lists are your secret weapon. A reusable check-list for typical outings can be a game-changer. Whether it's a digital list on your phone or a magnetic one on the fridge, having a visual reminder of what needs to be packed not only reduces stress but also helps in delegating tasks to other family members. Kids can get involved too, checking off items as they pack them, which fosters responsibility and teamwork (and maybe they'll stop asking you where their shoes are!).

Involving Everyone

Speaking of teamwork, involving the whole family in the planning process is crucial. It ensures that everyone's interests and needs are considered, making activities enjoyable for all. Plus, it saves you from hearing, 'But I didn't want to go hiking' for the millionth time. This can be as simple as having a family meeting to discuss ideas for the next outing or as organized as setting up a family suggestion box where everyone can drop their activity ideas. Regularly rotating who gets to pick the activity can keep things fair and exciting—because apparently, an 'elected rotational dictatorship' is the only thing that'll stop a mutiny over movie night! It turns planning into a collaborative, inclusive process rather than a parental decree.

By integrating these systems and strategies into your family life, you're not just streamlining the logistics—you're creating space for more joy and less chaos. It's okay if things don't always go perfectly because what matters most is the time spent together, not the flawless execution of the plan. Remember, every family outing, even with a few bumps, becomes a memory in your shared adventure. You're doing a fantastic job balancing everyone's needs, and by embracing these tools, you're not only making life easier for yourself but also fostering more connection and fun along the way. Keep going—you've got this!

Hey, come back with that checklist!
Why does this always happen when we're trying to get organized?
Let's see what activity we tackle next!
Looks like the cat has other plans!
ACT
Alright, let's just go with it!
HAHAHA~
ACT
With a bit of humor and flexibility, even the quirkiest organizational adventures can lead to success!
We did it—despite the chaos!

Chapter Checklist

☐ Set up a shared family calendar and invite all family members to join.

☐ Brainstorm and implement themed activity days.

☐ Create and laminate a generic outing check-list; place it where it's easily accessible.

☐ Hold a family meeting to discuss and plan the next month's activities, ensuring everyone contributes.

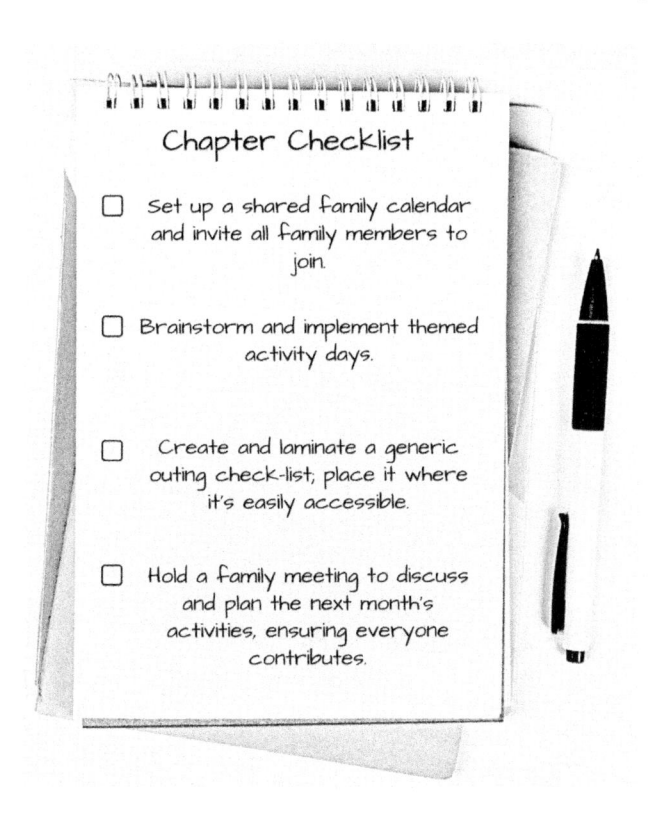

Bullet Point Summary

- Utilize shared digital calendars and family planning apps for synchronized scheduling.
- Simplify decision-making by setting themes for activities.
- Use check-lists to prepare for activities efficiently.
- Involve all family members in the planning process to ensure inclusivity and enjoyment.

CHAPTER 5.2

ADHD-FRIENDLY STRATEGIES FOR MANAGING CHILDREN'S SCHEDULES

Navigating the whimsical world of a child's schedule when ADHD is in the mix can sometimes feel like trying to pin the tail on a galloping donkey. It's a dynamic dance, full of unexpected twirls and dips. But what if we could choreograph this dance to a rhythm that both you and your child (AKA your little "donkey" or maybe sometimes your little 'the biblical word-for-donkey') can follow with ease? Enter the realm of visual schedules and flexible planning, where the chaotic becomes the curated, transforming daily routines into smooth, enjoyable experiences.

Visual Schedule Design

Let's start by painting the day with broad strokes of clarity using visual schedules. This method isn't just about writing down what needs to be done; it's about creating a visual map of the day that your child can easily understand and follow. For children, particularly those with ADHD, visual cues are like little beacons of guidance throughout the day. They help in transitioning between activities, reducing the anxiety that often comes with unexpected changes or decisions. You can use simple charts with symbols representing different activities—like a toothbrush for brushing teeth or a book for reading time. Or, for the tech-savvy, digital apps that provide interactive, customizable schedules can make this process even more engaging. The key here is consistency and visibility. Place these schedules where they're easily seen—on the refrigerator, by the bedroom door, or as a background on a tablet or computer they frequently use. This constant visual reminder helps internalize the routine, making it a natural part of the day rather than a series of surprises that could trigger resistance or meltdowns.

Flexibility in Scheduling

However, the plot twist in this narrative is the need for flexibility. As much as a consistent routine is beneficial, the unpredictable nature of ADHD—and, let's face it, life—means that rigidity can sometimes lead to more frustration. After all, if there's one thing ADHD excels at, it's turning 'sticking to the plan' into 'oops, I accidentally started a new project.' Thus, building flexibility into your child's schedule is crucial. This doesn't mean throwing the timetable out the window but rather allowing for buffers and 'choose your own adventure' options. For instance, after school, you might schedule an hour for your child to choose between several pre-approved activities like drawing, playing outside, or reading. This choice gives them a sense of control and ownership over their time, catering to their spontaneous nature in a structured way. Also, have backup plans ready for days when the usual schedule just isn't feasible. Maybe a planned outdoor activity isn't an option due to weather; having a quick indoor game or craft project on standby can save the day.

Use of Reminders and Alarms

To further ease the daily dance, incorporating reminders and alarms can act like the cues in a choreographed performance, guiding your child through their day without constant parental prompts. Technology can be a great ally here. Setting alarms on a phone, tablet, or even a smart home device can remind your child of transitions or upcoming tasks. For younger children, visual or auditory timers that signal the end of one activity and the start of another can help prepare them for the change, reducing tantrums or resistance. These little nudges help foster independence as children learn to follow their schedule and manage their time, which is a valuable skill as they grow.

Coordinating with Caregivers and Schools

Finally, ensuring that these rhythms extend beyond the home is essential. Consistency across environments significantly helps children with ADHD thrive. It's kind of like trying to stick to a diet but realizing your babysitter keeps offering your kid cookies every time you leave. Coordinate with caregivers, teachers, and other adults in your child's life to make sure there's a unified approach to schedules. Share the tools and methods that work well at home —perhaps the visual schedule or the specific reminders. Most schools and caregivers are willing to accommodate these strategies, especially when they see their positive impact. Regular meetings or updates can ensure everyone is on the same page, making the child feel supported and understood, no matter where they are.

By weaving these strategies into the fabric of your child's daily life, you not only ease the typical stressors associated with scheduling but also empower them to navigate their day with confidence and a sense of control. Remember, every time you adjust or introduce something new, you're giving them the tools to succeed on their own terms. It's not about perfection, but progress. You're transforming what might feel like a chaotic sprint into a graceful dance, where your child learns to move confidently through each day, one small step at a time. And through it all, know that you're helping them build a foundation of independence and resilience. Keep going—you're doing amazing work!

CHAPTER 5.2 | 175

Chapter Checklist

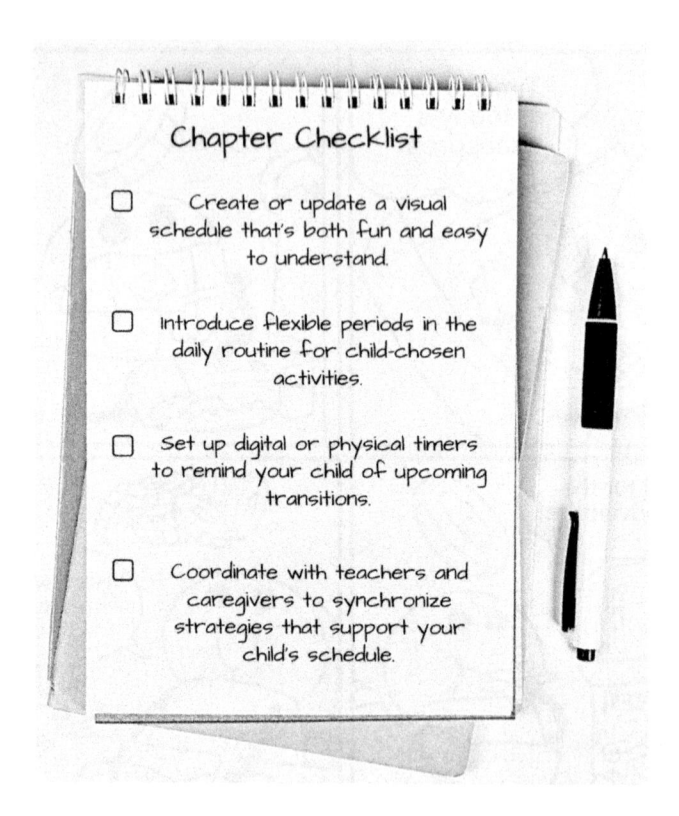

- ☐ Create or update a visual schedule that's both fun and easy to understand.

- ☐ Introduce flexible periods in the daily routine for child-chosen activities.

- ☐ Set up digital or physical timers to remind your child of upcoming transitions.

- ☐ Coordinate with teachers and caregivers to synchronize strategies that support your child's schedule.

Bullet Point Summary

- Use visual schedules for clear, engaging daily routines.
- Incorporate flexibility to adapt to the unpredictable nature of ADHD.
- Implement reminders and alarms to foster independence and time management.
- Ensure consistency across different caregiving environments to support the child's routine.

CHAPTER 5.3

CREATING ADHD-INCLUSIVE FAMILY ROUTINES

Imagine trying to create a dance routine where every family member has a different dance style. That's what setting up a routine in a family touched by ADHD can sometimes feel like. It's about finding a rhythm that everyone can groove to, even when the beats are off. This isn't just about keeping track of who needs to be where, but about creating a framework that reduces the daily "what's next?" chaos, stabilizes expectations, and cuts down the morning madness and bedtime battles.

Routine Building Blocks

The cornerstone of any ADHD-friendly family routine lies in three C's: consistency, clarity, and simplicity. Okay, you caught me; that last one wasn't a C...but an S is technically *two "c" s* all confused and on top of one another, not entirely unlike the ADHD family! Consistency means having predictable patterns that don't often change, like regular meal times, bedtimes, and wake-up times. This predictability can be soothing to an ADHD brain, reducing anxiety caused by uncertainty. Clarity involves clear expectations about what each part of the routine involves. This might mean having visual aids around the house that remind younger kids what they need to do to get ready for school or setting specific, simple steps for chores. Simplicity in your routine ensures that nobody feels overwhelmed. Overloading the day with activities or tasks can be a recipe for stress and frustration, especially for someone who might struggle with transitions or sensory overload.

Incorporating Choice and Control

Here's where it gets interesting: integrating choice and control can transform a mundane routine into something that everyone actually looks forward to. For family members with ADHD, who might often feel that they have little control over their impulsivity or distractibility, having a say in their routine can be empowering. This could mean letting your child choose their outfit (from preselected options to avoid morning meltdowns) or having a 'wild card' evening once a week where they can pick an activity for the family. Suppose you really want to aim for parent-of-the-decade status. In that case, you might keep the social norms—and the fear of being a social pariah—at bay when your child chooses pajama pants and a formal top. That wouldn't be too bad, except they might also decide it's "Opposite Day." After their will has been exercised and clothes are on, you'll be left wondering why they want it so dark "upstairs" and windy "downstairs." Sure, other parents might give you a side-eye, but allowing your child that choice will definitely earn you some points! Respecting these small decisions validates their feelings and preferences, fostering a sense of independence and self-esteem.

Adjusting Routines Over Time

Flexibility is your friend. As much as routines benefit from being consistent, they also need to evolve as your family grows and changes. I mean, what worked for your toddler isn't going to fly with your ten-year-old—unless they still love the idea of going to bed with a stuffed animal, lullaby, and maybe a round of peek-a-boo—in which case, good luck explaining that at a sleepover! Regularly taking the pulse of your family's needs and the effectiveness of your routine is crucial. Maybe your teen has started a new after-school program and needs to adjust their homework time, or perhaps you've started a new job that shifts meal times. These adjustments shouldn't feel like failures but rather natural evolutions of family life. Keeping the dialogue open about what's working and what isn't can help you tweak routines without upheaval.

Example Routines

Let's illustrate with some examples. Consider a morning routine that includes a check-list for each child that they tick off as they complete tasks—from brushing teeth to packing their school bag. This can be paired with a reward system, like earning points towards a weekend treat. Or a bedtime routine that starts with winding down activities an hour before sleep, limiting screens, and including calming activities like reading a story or having a warm bath. For weekends, a routine might be looser. Still, it could include a family activity in the morning, individual quiet time in the afternoon, and a family movie or game night.

Crafting ADHD-inclusive family routines isn't about rigidity; it's about creating a flexible structure that supports each family member's needs and growth. You're not aiming for perfection but progress—a routine that feels like a team effort, where everyone plays a part in keeping the rhythm going. It's about giving yourself grace on those days when everything doesn't go to plan and celebrating the small wins when things do. Remember, you're not just managing the chaos; you're helping your family find a groove that feels natural and supportive, allowing everyone to shine in their own way. You've got this, and each step forward is a victory.

Cereal is for eating, not wearing!
Just five more minutes, please!
BRUSH YOUR TEETH
Toothpaste goes on the brush, not the sink!
Why is finding matching socks so hard?
Everyone sit down and eat!
We did it! Ready for the day, team?
Lunchbox
Back Pack
With a bit of humor and teamwork, even the most chaotic mornings can start off right!

Chapter Checklist

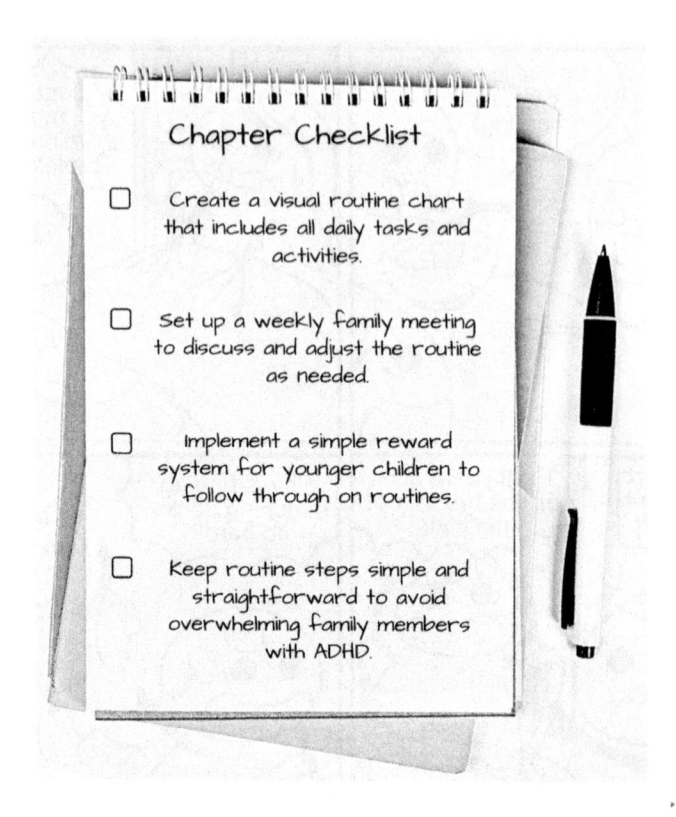

- [ ] Create a visual routine chart that includes all daily tasks and activities.

- [ ] Set up a weekly family meeting to discuss and adjust the routine as needed.

- [ ] Implement a simple reward system for younger children to follow through on routines.

- [ ] Keep routine steps simple and straightforward to avoid overwhelming family members with ADHD.

Bullet Point Summary

- Build routines based on consistency, clarity, and simplicity.
- Integrate choices to empower family members with ADHD.
- Regularly evaluate and adjust routines to fit changing family dynamics.
- Provide clear, visual reminders and incentives to support the routine.

CHAPTER 5.4

DECLUTTERING WITH KIDS: MAKING IT FUN AND ENGAGING

Gamification of Decluttering

Imagine turning the often dreaded task of decluttering into a game where every discarded toy is a point scored, and every neatly folded garment earns a badge of honor. Sounds fun, right? It's like 'Housework Olympics'—minus the medals, but hey, you might still win a gold star or, at the very least, not trip over LEGOs! This is precisely what gamification of decluttering is all about—transforming the mundane into the enjoyable, especially for kids who might see tidying up as a chore worse than the most boring homework. For children with ADHD, who might struggle with staying on task or who get easily overwhelmed by too many stimuli, turning decluttering into a game can significantly increase their engagement. Start by setting clear, achievable goals—like clearing out one drawer or organizing a shelf within a set time limit—and add an element of competition by using a timer. Who can beat the clock? Offer rewards that don't necessarily have to be material; they could be an extra half hour of bedtime stories or their choice of movie on family night. This approach not only makes decluttering less intimidating but also teaches valuable organizational skills in a fun and memorable way.

Regular Decluttering Sessions

Incorporating regular decluttering sessions into your family's routine can transform this task from an overwhelming, chaotic ordeal into a manageable, even enjoyable routine. Think of it like dental hygiene—it's better to clean regularly than wait for a problem to arise. Establish a decluttering schedule that suits your family's rhythm, perhaps every Sunday afternoon or the first Saturday of every month. Make it a family affair where everyone participates, sorting their belongings into keep, donate, or throw away categories. Playing upbeat music during these sessions or creating a family decluttering playlist can add an element of fun and keep everyone motivated. Throwing in occasional humorous and encouraging statements with a sincere smile goes a long way, too. Kind of like, "Wow! I've never seen so much of your floor before! Well done!" Over time, these regular sessions will not only keep your home tidier but also instill a habit of regular review and letting go of unneeded items, which is particularly beneficial for children with ADHD, helping them manage their environment and, by extension, their mental space.

Teaching Organizational Skills

"Decluttering offers a perfect opportunity to teach children essential organizational skills in a hands-on manner. And hey, you can introduce the 'One In, One Out' rule—because if you don't, you'll soon be living in a LEGO fortress with no way out. This rule helps maintain balance and prevents clutter from taking over like an army of forgotten toys. Engage your children in setting up systems that work for them, perhaps color-coding their drawers or categorizing their toys into bins. Visual systems work particularly well as they provide clear, external cues that children with ADHD find helpful. For instance, using different colored bins for different types of toys or labels with pictures for younger children who are not yet reading can be effective. Let them decide what goes where, giving them a sense of control and ownership over their space, which can be empowering and encourage them to maintain the system."

Celebrating Success

After each decluttering session, take a moment to celebrate your family's success. Maybe it's enjoying a small treat together or just standing in the newly cleaned space, pretending you're on a home makeover show—cue the slow-motion reveal! Celebrations reinforce positive behavior and make the effort feel worthwhile. They also help build a positive association with decluttering, turning it into a rewarding activity rather than a dreaded chore. For children with ADHD, who may struggle with long-term motivation, these immediate, positive reinforcements are particularly important. They serve as tangible reminders of what can be accomplished with teamwork and effort, boosting their self-esteem and motivation.

Through these strategies, decluttering transforms from a daunting task into an engaging, educational activity that not only keeps your home organized but also builds lasting skills and positive behaviors in children, especially those with ADHD. Remember, you're not just tidying up a room—you're creating an environment that nurtures independence and teaches valuable life skills. By making decluttering a regular, fun, and rewarding part of family life, you're helping your child manage the typical chaos in a way that feels empowering rather than overwhelming. Each session is a step toward creating a space where your family can thrive, and that's something to celebrate!

Chapter Checklist

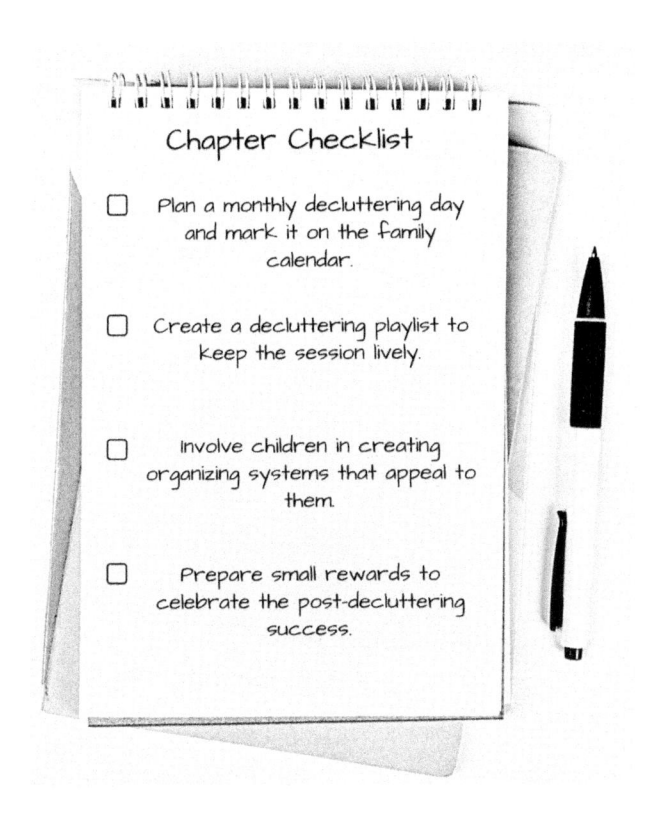

☐ Plan a monthly decluttering day and mark it on the family calendar.

☐ Create a decluttering playlist to keep the session lively.

☐ Involve children in creating organizing systems that appeal to them.

☐ Prepare small rewards to celebrate the post-decluttering success.

Bullet Point Summary

- Turn decluttering into a game with timed challenges and rewards.
- Establish a regular decluttering schedule involving the whole family.
- Teach organizational skills through practical involvement and fun systems.
- Celebrate successes to reinforce positive behavior and outcomes.

CHAPTER 5.5

MANAGING FAMILY EXPECTATIONS AND RESPONSIBILITIES

Navigating family expectations and responsibilities can be akin to walking a tightrope while juggling—doable, yes, but oh, so tricky, especially when ADHD is in the mix. Clear and open communication becomes your safety net, ensuring that everyone in the family understands what's expected of them and what they can expect from others. It's about being as transparent as possible, especially when discussing the complexities ADHD might bring into family dynamics. This might mean sitting down for a family meeting where you openly discuss how ADHD affects daily interactions and responsibilities. It's about saying, "Hey, this is what I'm grappling with," and "Here's how we can tackle this together." Such discussions can help demystify ADHD for those who don't experience it, fostering a deeper understanding and stronger familial bonds.

Role assignments in a family work best when they play to each member's strengths. For instance, if your ADHD makes you great at brainstorming fun ideas but less stellar at executing detailed plans, maybe you're the CFO ('Chief Fun Officer'), coming up with wild adventures. At the same time, someone else, like your super-organized partner, can figure out how to actually make it happen—because, let's be honest, if you planned the whole thing, you'd probably end up at a museum when the goal was a beach day. This way, everyone contributes in ways that make them feel competent and valuable, reducing frustrations and mismatched expectations. It's about crafting a family team where each member's roles and responsibilities are tailored, not just to their capabilities but also to their challenges. This consideration ensures that no one is set up for failure but is instead positioned for success.

Negotiating compromises is another critical dance step in the choreography of family life. It's about finding the middle ground where everyone feels heard and valued. When conflicts arise—and they will—approach them with a mindset of finding solutions rather than assigning blame. Use phrases like, "I see your point, how about we try…" to keep the dialogue constructive. Remember, the goal is not to win but to reach an understanding that respects everyone's needs. This approach is fundamental in families touched by ADHD, where impulsivity and emotional dysregulation can sometimes lead to fiery exchanges. Keeping the communication lines open and flexible allows for smoother resolutions and maintains peace.

Establishing support systems within the family that acknowledge and address ADHD-related challenges is like building a scaffold around a fragile sapling—it provides the support needed for growth despite the storms. It's kind of like giving everyone a secret signal to call a time-out, but instead of refereeing a basketball game, you're avoiding an emotional meltdown because someone misplaced their shoes again… for the third time. This might involve setting up routines that help manage ADHD symptoms or having a designated quiet space where family members can go to regroup when things get overwhelming. It can also mean agreeing on signals or codes that convey 'I need a break' or 'I'm feeling overwhelmed,' which can be especially useful in preventing meltdowns or arguments before they start. These systems aren't just practical; they are affirmations of your family's commitment to supporting each other, reinforcing the understanding that everyone's challenges are important.

By integrating these strategies into your family life, you're not just navigating the challenges of ADHD—you're building a home where everyone feels seen, heard, and valued. Clear expectations and supportive roles foster a sense of belonging where each family member can shine in their own way. Remember, it's not about perfection but about progress, where compromises are embraced, and every effort, no matter how small, is celebrated. You're creating a space where challenges are met with understanding, and love and encouragement become the foundation for every interaction. You've got this!

Alright, let's divide the chores for the week.
How did Whiskers get all the chores?
dishes
vacuum
laundry
If you get two extra turns, we get to choose the game!
Okay, but I get three extra turns and no cleaning for a week!
Deal! Now, let's play!
This is the best game night ever!
With a bit of humor and flexibility, family dynamics and organization can lead to fun and memorable moments!

Chapter Checklist

☐ Schedule regular family meetings to discuss roles, expectations, and challenges.

☐ Assign tasks and responsibilities that align with each family member's strengths and needs.

☐ Practice conflict resolution techniques that focus on compromise and understanding.

☐ Implement family support mechanisms like quiet zones or signal codes for stress management.

Bullet Point Summary

- Foster clear and open communication to manage expectations and responsibilities effectively.
- Assign roles based on individual strengths and challenges, accommodating ADHD traits.
- Negotiate compromises to resolve conflicts, focusing on empathy and understanding.
- Establish supportive systems within the family to help manage ADHD-related challenges.

CHAPTER 5.6

COPING WITH MULTI-TASKING CHALLENGES IN FAMILY LIFE

In the whirlwind of family life, trying to juggle multiple tasks simultaneously can often feel like spinning plates while standing on a unicycle. Especially for those of us navigating the waves of ADHD, multi-tasking isn't just challenging; it can be a recipe for increased anxiety and inefficiency. That's why honing a single-tasking focus can feel less like a circus act and more like a serene ballet, each movement deliberate and effective.

Single-Tasking Focus

The art of single-tasking isn't just about doing one thing at a time; it's about immersing yourself fully in the task at hand, giving it your complete attention. Failing to do so is like trying to eat spaghetti while also folding laundry—trust me, sauce ends up where it shouldn't. This can be a game-changer in reducing the overwhelm that often accompanies multi-tasking. For example, during family meal times, focus solely on enjoying the meal and engaging with your family without the distraction of phones or television. This not only improves the quality of family interactions but also helps everyone feel more connected. Single-tasking allows you to perform better, as each task gets your undivided attention, reducing mistakes that happen when you're trying to do too much at once. It's about quality over quantity, doing less but doing it better.

Tools to Manage Tasks

To effectively reduce the cognitive load of multi-tasking, several tools and apps can be your allies. Task management apps like Asana or Trello allow you to organize tasks into boards and lists, making it easy to focus on one thing at a time. I mean, let's face it, the alternative is trying to remember everything and ending up at the grocery store with no list, wondering why you're holding a pineapple and lightbulbs. You can set up different boards for various aspects of family life—like household chores, grocery shopping, or family projects. Each board can contain lists for specific tasks, and each task can be tackled individually without the chaos of trying to keep everything in your head or juggling multiple activities simultaneously. These tools help clear your mental space by keeping track of what needs to be done so you can focus entirely on the task at hand without worrying about forgetting something important.

Setting Realistic Limits

Part of effective task management is knowing your limits. It's crucial to set realistic expectations about what you can achieve in a given period, particularly in a family setting where needs and priorities can be diverse and demanding. Think of it like this: You can try to do five things at once, but you'll probably end up halfway through folding laundry, realizing the oven's on, and wondering why you're holding a stapler. Did your clothes really do something to deserve such a smoky, stapled fate? Or is it possible you tried to take on too much at once or even committed to too much at once? This might mean acknowledging that you can realistically only commit to one or two major tasks per day outside of routine family activities. Communicate these limits clearly with your family, setting an example that it's okay to say no or to defer tasks when necessary. This not only helps prevent burnout but also teaches your children the importance of setting and respecting their own limits.

Mindfulness Techniques

Incorporating mindfulness techniques into your daily routine can significantly enhance your ability to focus on one task at a time. Simple practices like mindful breathing or taking a moment to center yourself before starting a new task can help clear your mind of distractions. You might start a family habit where everyone takes three deep breaths together before beginning a meal or a family activity. This not only helps in reducing stress but also models healthy ways to handle multi-tasking anxiety. Mindfulness fosters a present-moment awareness, making you more attuned to the task at hand and less likely to get pulled into multi-tasking habits.

By shifting from multi-tasking to a more focused, single-tasking approach, you create a ripple effect of calm and clarity in your home. I know it's hard to break the habit of trying to do everything at once, but remember, it's okay to slow down and pay full attention to one thing at a time. You're not just getting more done; you're showing your family that balance is possible, even in the chaos. Take each task as it comes, and trust that the calm you create for yourself will resonate with everyone around you. You've got this. One task––one slice of chaos––one step at a time.

198 | EFFORTLESS ADHD ORGANIZATION

Chapter Checklist

- ☐ Choose one family meal this week to practice single-tasking with all electronics away.

- ☐ Set up a task management app to organize this week's family activities.

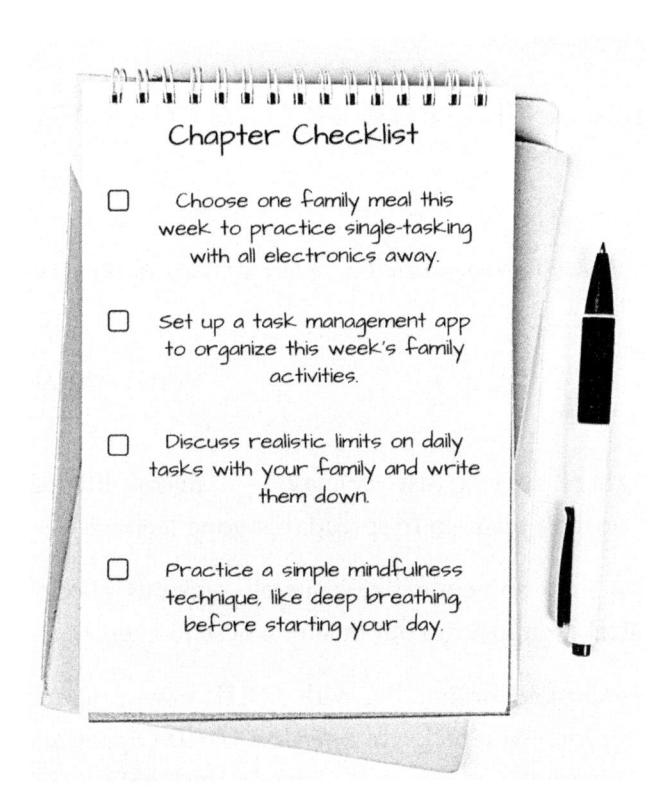

- ☐ Discuss realistic limits on daily tasks with your family and write them down.

- ☐ Practice a simple mindfulness technique, like deep breathing, before starting your day.

Bullet Point Summary

- Embrace single-tasking to improve focus and reduce stress.
- Utilize task management tools to organize and separate tasks effectively.
- Set realistic limits on the number of tasks to handle simultaneously.
- Practice mindfulness techniques to enhance focus and present-moment awareness.

UNLOCK THE POWER OF GENEROSITY

"The best way to find yourself is to lose yourself in the service of others."

— MAHATMA GANDHI

Helping others doesn't just feel good—it makes life better for everyone. So, let's team up to spread that good feeling!

Would you help someone like yourself—curious about how to tackle ADHD organization but unsure where to begin?

My goal is to make organizing with ADHD easy, fun, and stress-free for everyone who picks up *Effortless ADHD Organization*. But I can't reach everyone on my own—I need your help!

People often decide which book to try based on reviews from readers just like you. So, I'm asking for a quick yet *vital* favor: Would you take a moment to leave a review? It costs nothing and only takes a minute, but it could make a *huge* difference for someone struggling to get organized.

Your review might help…

- …one more person get control over their daily chaos.
- …one more overwhelmed parent balance family and work.
- …one more young adult navigate the challenges of ADHD.
- …one more person discover simple, affordable ways to make life easier.

It's easy to help: just scan the QR code below and leave a review. Your kind words might be the boost someone else who needs to get started on their own journey

If you love helping others, then you're my kind of person. Thank you so much for being part of this mission!

With heaps of gratitude,

Sterling Cheney

PART VI

ADHD IN THE WORKPLACE

Imagine walking into a buzzing office or your charming but chaotic home workspace. Picture the desk: a battleground of paperwork, coffee mugs, half-finished projects, and that one pen that never works. Now, what if I told you that this seemingly benign chaos could actually be your secret weapon? With a sprinkle of creativity, a dash of organization, and a good dose of humor, transforming your work desk from a cluttered mess to a productivity palace is not just possible—it's going to be fun. Welcome to the ADHD-friendly way of conquering workspace chaos.

CHAPTER 6.1

ORGANIZING YOUR WORK DESK FOR MAXIMUM EFFICIENCY

Let's start with the real estate of any professional or personal command center: the desk. Optimizing your desk's layout isn't just about making it look pretty; it's about creating a space that minimizes distractions and maximizes your unique way of working. And let's be honest, if your desk looks anything like mine, it's less 'command center' and more 'where did that sandwich come from?' Imagine segments on your desk like zones in a game—each zone dedicated to a type of work or activity. You might have a 'command zone' right at the center for your computer and essential work tools, a 'quick access zone' within arm's reach for frequently used items, and a 'deep work zone' perhaps with a secondary monitor or a dedicated writing space that allows you to dive deep without distractions.

Now, onto the tools of the trade. Every craftsperson has their toolkit, and for those of us with ADHD, this toolkit can be a game-changer. Consider using document holders to keep important papers at eye level, reducing the physical clutter that can often invade our mental workspace. Task boards, either physical or digital, can be a visual and interactive way to keep track of your projects. Tools that sync across your devices, like cloud-based task management applications, ensure that you can capture ideas and tasks on the go, never losing a flash of inspiration or forgetting a sudden meeting again.

Personalizing your workspace with items that reduce stress and maintain focus can also turn your desk into a haven of productivity. Whether it's a stress ball, a fidget spinner, or even a plant, find something that calms you down or helps you focus. Just don't go overboard with the plants—you want to boost your productivity, not turn your desk into a scene from *Jumanji*. There's nothing more distracting than having a giant plant come to life and try to throttle you while trying to finish that graphic design project before deadline! Remember, the goal is to create a space that feels both comforting and stimulating, aligning with your ADHD brain's need for sensory balance.

Routine desk clean-up might not sound thrilling, but think of it as a reset button for your productivity. Establishing a simple, daily clean-up strategy—like a five-minute tidy-up before lunch or at the end of the day—can help keep chaos at bay and ensure your desk remains a place where creativity flows, not flounders.

Transforming your workspace with these ADHD-friendly strategies doesn't just mean you'll find your pens more easily (though that's a definite plus). It's about creating a space where you can focus, feel empowered, and finally work in a way that aligns with how your brain operates best. Give yourself the grace to try new setups and adapt as needed—your desk is a living space, just like you are. With each tweak and adjustment, you're not just organizing your desk; you're setting yourself up to thrive. You've got this, and you deserve to feel at home in your workspace!

Time to tackle this paperwork beast!
J
Take that, chaos!
You're next, digital mess!
Routine to the rescue!
ROUTINE
Order achieved and sustained!
J
ROUTINE
You missed a spot!
There's always a next battle!
ROUTINE
With the right tools and strategies, even the fiercest Chaos Monsters can be tamed, making organization sustainable and fun!

Chapter Checklist

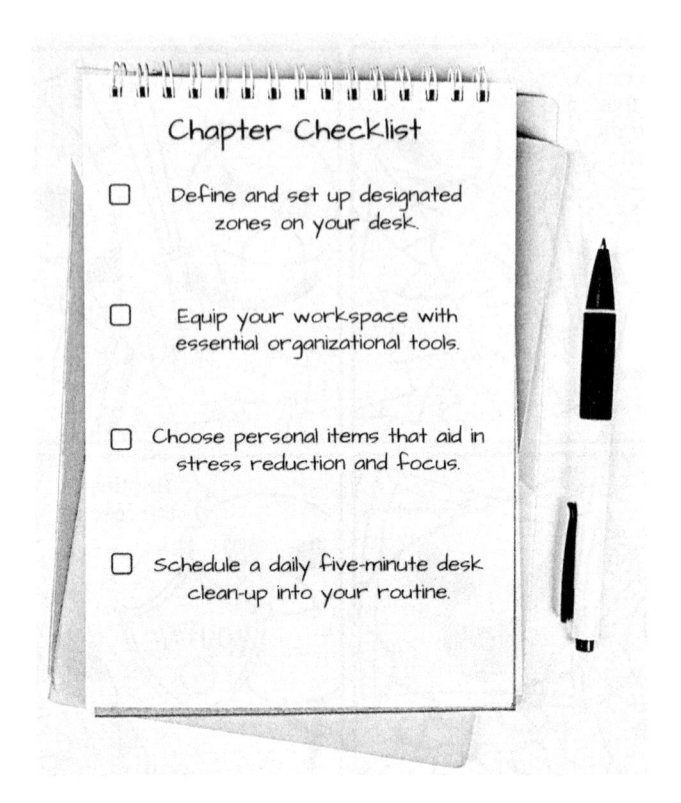

- ☐ Define and set up designated zones on your desk.
- ☐ Equip your workspace with essential organizational tools.
- ☐ Choose personal items that aid in stress reduction and focus.
- ☐ Schedule a daily five-minute desk clean-up into your routine.

Bullet Point Summary

- Designate work zones on your desk for different tasks.
- Utilize organizational tools like document holders and task boards.
- Personalize your space with items that help maintain focus.
- Implement a simple daily desk clean-up routine.

CHAPTER 6.2

HANDLING WORK-RELATED STRESS WITH ORGANIZATIONAL TECHNIQUES

So, let's chat about a not-so-fun topic that's probably as unwelcome as that one overzealous telemarketer: work-related stress. Yes, it's the uninvited plus-one that somehow always finds its way into our careers, particularly when you're spinning more plates than a circus performer, courtesy of ADHD. But here's the kicker: with some clever prioritization and organizational jazz, you can play that stress like a sexy saxophone instead of letting it play you.

First up, let's tackle prioritization. It's a bit like deciding which fires to put out when everything seems ablaze. Prioritizing tasks effectively can drastically cut down your stress levels by helping you control your workload and set realistic expectations. How? By identifying what needs immediate attention and what can wait. Think of it as being the director of your own work-life movie; you decide what scene gets shot next based on the script's demand, not on the whims of the chaotic supporting actors. For instance, that presentation for next week's client meeting? That's your headline act. Meanwhile, the weekly inventory check that's due in ten days can take a backstage seat for now.

Now, let's move on to some stress-reducing rituals because sometimes, you need more than just good intentions to keep the stress monsters at bay. Simple mindfulness exercises can be your secret weapon here. Picture this: Before diving into a daunting task or after a turbo-charged meeting, you take five minutes to do a breathing exercise or a quick meditative session right at your desk. It's like hitting the reset button, giving your brain a fresh start— that's *way* better than when your computer freezes, and you have no idea what happened, so you just shut it off and pray. Apps like Headspace offer guided sessions that fit neatly into these short slots. They are perfect for reining in runaway stress levels before they gallop off.

But what about the tools? Oh, the sweet, sweet arsenal of organizational tools! Project management software, like Asana or Monday.com, doesn't just keep your tasks neatly lined up; they're like having an overview map of the battlefield. They allow you to track deadlines, collaborate seamlessly with your teammates, and visually break down massive projects into manageable tasks. No more feeling lost in the sauce of confusion and last-minute panics. With everything mapped out, you can see the forest for the trees— or, in work speak, the deadlines for the tasks!

Setting realistic goals is another cornerstone of keeping your work stress in check. It's about knowing your limits and communicating them clearly to your supervisors. There's bravery in telling your team leader, "Hey, to do my best work, I need a little more time on this project." This clarity not only sets you up for actual achievable successes but also aligns team expectations, reducing the friction that mismatched expectations can create. It's about working smarter, not just harder, and ensuring that your capabilities and your commitments do a beautiful tango together rather than stepping on each other's toes.

Navigating workplace stress with ADHD might sound daunting, but with these strategies, you're not just surviving—you're setting up shop to thrive. It's about taking the bull by the horns, or in this case, the stress by the deadlines, and showing it who's boss. You're stronger and more capable than you might realize, and it's okay to take things step by step. With your organizational toolkit in one hand and your stress-busting strategies in the other, you're well-equipped to turn what could be a stress fest into just another day at the office—a productive, manageable, and, yes, even enjoyable one. So go ahead, take that deep breath, and let's get your workday back under your command. You've got this! One task at a time, one victory at a time.

With a bit of humor and the right techniques, even the biggest Work Stress giant can be tamed and turned into a peaceful ally!

Chapter Checklist

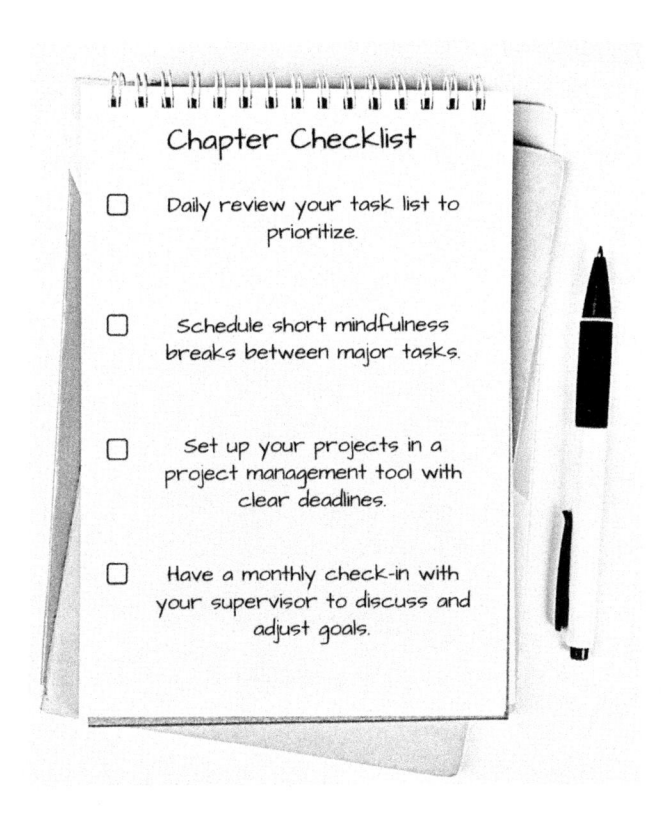

☐ Daily review your task list to prioritize.

☐ Schedule short mindfulness breaks between major tasks.

☐ Set up your projects in a project management tool with clear deadlines.

☐ Have a monthly check-in with your supervisor to discuss and adjust goals.

Bullet Point Summary

- Prioritize tasks to manage workload effectively.
- Use mindfulness exercises to reset stress levels.
- Implement project management tools for a clear overview of tasks.
- Set and communicate realistic goals to align expectations.

CHAPTER 6.3

NAVIGATING OFFICE POLITICS AND INTERPERSONAL RELATIONSHIPS

Navigating the choppy waters of office politics and managing interpersonal relationships at work can sometimes feel like you're playing a board game where everyone else has the rule book except you—especially when your ADHD brain processes social cues and office dynamics in its own unique way. But here's a little secret: understanding the social dynamics at your workplace and mastering a few strategic communication techniques can turn what often feels like a minefield into a manageable, if not enjoyable, part of your professional life.

Let's dive into the social dynamics first. Office politics often get a bad rap, but at their core, they're really about understanding the informal networks and power structures within your workplace. It's about knowing who the decision-makers are, what the unspoken rules of engagement are, and how decisions are really made. For someone with ADHD, who might miss subtle cues or feel overwhelmed by multiple social interactions, this can seem daunting—like trying to read a room when you're not even sure where the door is. However, breaking it down into observable patterns and behaviors can help. Start by being a keen observer. Who aligns with whom? What communication styles are rewarded? How are successes and failures discussed? This isn't about changing who you are; it's about understanding the playing field. Think of it as gathering intel for a mission. The more you understand the dynamics, the better you can navigate them without compromising your authenticity—just don't expect an actual spy gadget budget!

Effective communication is your best tool here. It's not just about what you say but how you say it. Clear, concise communication can cut through a lot of the noise that comes with ADHD. When expressing your needs or ideas, be direct and straightforward. Before a meeting, take a few minutes to outline your thoughts so you can stay on track. If you're worried about forgetting, it's perfectly okay to bring a notepad or use a digital device to keep notes. This can also help in clarifying your thoughts if you need to revisit them during a discussion. Remember, the goal is to convey your thoughts in a way that's not just heard but understood.

Building a support network at work can sometimes feel like trying to make friends at a crowded concert. Everyone's shouting, but you're just hoping someone else also knows the lyrics. Start by identifying allies—colleagues who share similar values or work ethics. These connections can provide emotional support and help you navigate those complex social situations, like decoding why Karen always sends cryptic emails. Plus, never underestimate the power of a good work friend; they can turn even the most awkward office politics into a backstage pass for survival.

When it comes to handling conflicts, think of it as strategic diplomacy. Conflicts are inevitable, but with a bit of planning, they can often be managed effectively. Start by keeping your emotions in check. It's easy to react in the heat of the moment, especially when your ADHD impulsivity kicks in. Take a breath, step back, and approach the situation with a problem-solving mindset. Articulate your perspective clearly and listen actively to the other side. This doesn't just show respect but often opens up pathways to resolution that you might have yet to consider.

As you weave these strategies into your daily work life, remember that you're learning to navigate a world that might feel confusing at times, but you have all the tools to succeed. It's okay if things don't fall into place perfectly right away. Each day brings new opportunities to practice and refine these skills. With observation, clear communication, strategic alliances, and a cool head in conflicts, you're not just managing office dynamics; you're mastering them in a way that works uniquely for you. You've got this, and your ability to grow through these challenges is something to be proud of every step of the way!

218 | EFFORTLESS ADHD ORGANIZATION

Chapter Checklist

- ☐ Spend a week observing and noting office dynamics and interactions.

- ☐ Practice transparent communication by summarizing your main points before meetings.

- ☐ Identify at least two potential allies in your workplace.

- ☐ Develop a personal strategy for handling conflicts, including a step-back moment to assess the best response.

Bullet Point Summary

- Understand and observe office dynamics.
- Communicate clearly and effectively.
- Build and rely on a supportive network.
- Approach conflicts with a problem-solving attitude.

CHAPTER 6.4

TIME MANAGEMENT TIPS FOR MEETINGS AND DEADLINES

Imagine you're juggling, not just any juggling, but juggling with flaming torches. Now someone's throwing in a chainsaw named 'Urgent Meeting' and a kitten called 'Project Deadline.' Welcome to the ADHD work life, where meetings and deadlines can feel just a tad overwhelming. But hang tight, I've got some tricks up my sleeve to turn that anxiety-inducing circus act into a well-orchestrated ballet.

First off, let's tackle those meetings that can be as draining as a marathon. I mean, sometimes it feels like by the end, you're not sure if you've been in a meeting or survived a TED Talk on small talk. Making meetings more efficient isn't just about cutting down the time; it's about ensuring that every minute counts. Here's a game changer: a clear, concise agenda. This is your meeting blueprint. Before any meeting, draft an agenda that outlines the topics to be discussed, oh, and make it as specific as possible. This isn't just a to-do list; it's a roadmap that will guide your meeting from wandering off into the wilderness of tangents. Distribute this agenda before the meeting so everyone comes prepared, not just with ideas but with focused contributions. And here's a little secret—time each agenda item. Yes, it might feel a bit like putting a leash on your free-flowing discussions, but trust me, it keeps the wild beast of prolonged, pointless chatter at bay.

Now, while a good agenda sets the stage, keeping track of time during the meeting ensures you stick to the script. Appoint a timekeeper, or hey, take on the role yourself. This person's job isn't just to watch the clock; it's to gently steer the meeting back on course when the winds of digression blow too strong. And here's the kicker: always, always end with clearly defined follow-up actions. Who's doing what? By when? These closing notes are like the final scene of a great movie—they leave everyone satisfied and clear about the sequel.

Switching gears, let's talk deadlines—the bread and butter of workplace productivity, and often the bane of the ADHD experience. It's like they sneak up on you like ninjas when you swore they were still a week away. Managing these deadlines isn't just about hard work; it's about smart tactics. Break down each project into manageable tasks. This isn't groundbreaking, but here's where it gets good: visualize these tasks. Use a whiteboard, a digital tool, or even sticky notes on your wall—whatever helps turn the chaos into something you can see. Each task becomes a stepping stone rather than a mountain. And as you complete each one, take it down or mark it off. Honestly, there's nothing more satisfying than ripping down a sticky note like you're vanquishing a tiny paper foe—it keeps the momentum going!

Procrastination—the arch-nemesis of deadline management. Here's a strategy straight from the ADHD playbook: the power of immediate rewards. Break your project into chunks and assign a small reward for completing each chunk. Maybe it's a coffee break, a short walk, or an episode of your favorite show. Whatever floats your boat. The trick is to align these rewards with milestones. It's about making progress visible and rewarding, tapping directly into the ADHD brain's reward center.

Meetings and deadlines don't have to be the monsters under your professional bed. With these strategies, you can tame them, make them work for you, and maybe, just maybe, make your workday a bit more like that ballet—graceful, disciplined, and on point. I know it can feel like you're juggling flaming torches and kittens, but remember, you're stronger and more capable than you give yourself credit for. I'm so proud of you for taking steps to manage your workload in a way that suits you. You've got the creativity and determination to turn chaos into choreography. So, grab your agenda, your timer, and your reward chocolate bar, and let's turn those flaming torches and kittens into a performance worth a standing ovation. You've got this, and you're going to make it look effortless.

224 | EFFORTLESS ADHD ORGANIZATION

Chapter Checklist

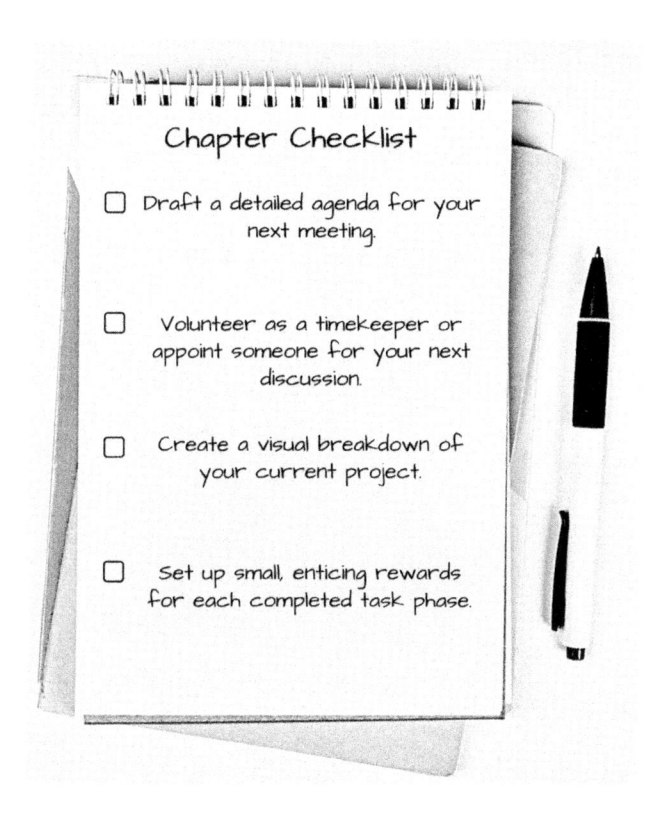

☐ Draft a detailed agenda for your next meeting.

☐ Volunteer as a timekeeper or appoint someone for your next discussion.

☐ Create a visual breakdown of your current project.

☐ Set up small, enticing rewards for each completed task phase.

Bullet Point Summary

- Use a detailed agenda with timed items for efficient meetings.
- Keep track of time actively during discussions.
- Ensure clear follow-up actions are noted at the end of each meeting.
- Break down projects into visual, manageable tasks for better deadline management.
- Use immediate rewards to combat procrastination effectively.

CHAPTER 6.5

CREATING AN ADHD-FRIENDLY WORKFLOW

Picture this: your workflow is like a river. For many, it's a smooth sail down a lazy river, but for those of us with ADHD, it often feels more like white-water rafting, unpredictably fast then suddenly calm, thrilling yet potentially chaotic. Crafting a workflow that caters to this unique rhythm isn't just helpful—it's crucial for maintaining sanity and productivity. Let's dive into how we can sculpt a workflow that not only understands but also celebrates your ADHD brain.

The first step is embracing visual task management systems. Why visual, you ask? Well, because our brains, with their ADHD flair, tend to process visual information more effectively than text alone. It's like giving a kid a picture book instead of a novel—it just clicks better. Plus, let's be honest; moving colorful sticky notes around a board is way more fun than trying to keep track of a to-do list buried somewhere in your phone—you might actually stick with it this time! Implement tools like Kanban boards, either physical with sticky notes or digital like Trello, where tasks can be moved around with a satisfying drag-and-drop. This method not only helps in tracking the progress of your work but also gives you a clear, immediate visual snapshot of where everything stands. Color-code these tasks—maybe red for urgent, blue for ongoing, green for done. It turns your workflow into a living canvas, not just a boring check-list.

However, a rigid workflow is like a tight pair of jeans—restrictive and uncomfortable. Flexibility is your friend. It's about creating a workflow that bends without breaking, accommodating the ebb and flow of your energy levels and attention span. Some days, you're a productivity powerhouse; other days, it's a struggle to just sift through emails. On those slower days, adjust your workflow to tackle lighter tasks, perhaps those that require less cognitive lift, leaving the heavy-lifting for your more focused days. This isn't slacking—it's strategic energy management, ensuring you remain productive without burning out.

Now, let's talk tech—specifically, technologies that minimize distractions. With the myriad of pings, rings, and dings around, it's easy to get sidetracked. I mean, sometimes I'll open my email, and 20 minutes later, I'm watching a YouTube video on how to fold a fitted sheet (still don't know how). Apps like Forest help keep your focus by gamifying attention—stay focused, and you grow a virtual tree; get distracted, and it withers. So, no pressure, but you're basically keeping a tiny digital forest alive. For those who find themselves drowning in a sea of open tabs, tools like OneTab can consolidate them into a single list, reducing clutter and freeing up mental space.

Regular adjustments to your workflow are like regular check-ups for your car—it keeps everything running smoothly. Set a recurring appointment with yourself, maybe once a month, to review your workflow. Is it still effective? What's working and what's not? Perhaps you've realized that the Kanban board is excellent, but the colors are getting confusing, or maybe the Forest app is fun, but you need something less whimsical. This is your chance to tweak tools, switch strategies, or introduce something entirely new. Remember, the goal is to ensure your workflow remains a well-oiled machine, tailored to your evolving needs and challenges.

As you stitch these elements together, you transform your workflow from a source of stress to a structured yet flexible framework that not only accommodates your ADHD but also plays to its strengths. I know it hasn't always been easy, but you've shown incredible resilience in adapting your methods to suit your unique rhythm. Your willingness to embrace new tools and adjust your strategies shows just how committed you are to making this work for you. Remember, it's okay to have days where the energy ebbs—you're learning to flow with it rather than fight against it. You're turning what many see as a disadvantage into your secret productivity weapon, crafting a day-to-day that feels less like battling rapids and more like skillfully navigating a river that's flowing just right for you.

230 | EFFORTLESS ADHD ORGANIZATION

Chapter Checklist

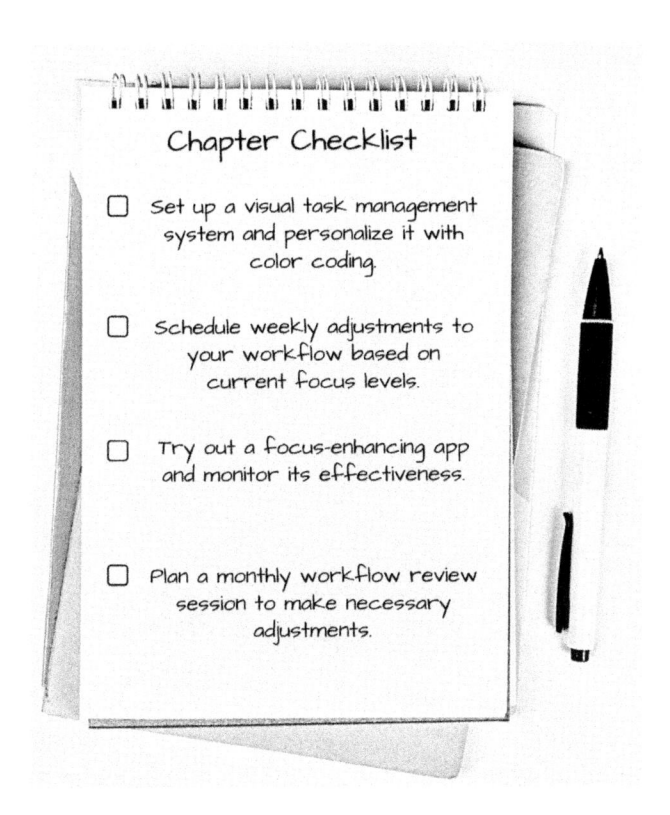

- [ ] Set up a visual task management system and personalize it with color coding.

- [ ] Schedule weekly adjustments to your workflow based on current focus levels.

- [ ] Try out a focus-enhancing app and monitor its effectiveness.

- [ ] Plan a monthly workflow review session to make necessary adjustments.

Bullet Point Summary

- Utilize visual task management systems to enhance cognitive processing.
- Maintain flexibility in your workflow to match varying energy and focus levels.
- Implement distraction-minimizing technologies to enhance concentration.
- Regularly assess and adjust your workflow to keep it effective.

CHAPTER 6.6

CAREER ADVANCEMENT: LEVERAGING ORGANIZATIONAL SKILLS FOR SUCCESS

Imagine yourself stepping into a performance review or career planning session, not with trepidation but with a secret arsenal of organizational superpowers that you're ready to unveil. Yes, your ADHD might have made the journey here a bit windy, but it's also packed your toolkit with some unique skills that can help you stand out in the workplace. It's about flipping the script—transforming potential ADHD challenges into professional strengths.

Firstly, let's talk about showcasing your organizational prowess during those all-important performance reviews. Here's where your ability to manage chaos—a skill honed from navigating daily life with ADHD—shines as a strategic asset. Start by documenting your projects and tasks systematically. Yes, those color-coded task lists or detailed project boards you've been maintaining? They're not just personal tools; they're proof of your ability to handle complexity. And let's face it, if you can keep track of a mind that's like a web browser with 30 tabs open, managing a complex project is right up your alley. Bring examples of how your unique methods have driven projects to completion or how your innovative organizing systems have improved team efficiency. It's about painting a picture that highlights your strengths in turning potential ADHD-induced chaos into productive outcomes.

Networking, often seen as just schmoozing and small talk, can actually be structured in a way that feels less daunting and more productive. Think of it as organizing your professional community. Start with a simple system to manage your contacts—perhaps a digital tool that allows you to note down how you met, key information about the contact, and when you last touched base. This approach not only keeps your connections fresh but also makes follow-ups timely and meaningful. When you reach out, make it count. Share an article you think they'd love, or congratulate them on a recent professional achievement. It's these personalized touches that turn networking from a chore into a genuine part of your career growth strategy.

Now, onto seizing those professional development opportunities. With your ADHD, you've likely developed a knack for continuous learning—after all, adapting various strategies to manage daily tasks requires constant tweaking and learning. And let's face it, who else could turn a simple search for a recipe into a three-hour deep dive on the origins of pasta? Use this innate curiosity to your advantage. Identify courses, workshops, or webinars that not only interest you but also enhance your organizational prowess. Perhaps a time management workshop or a seminar on innovative project management tools. Each of these learning opportunities not only adds to your skill set but also demonstrates your commitment to improving and staying relevant in your field.

Long-term career planning might seem a bit overwhelming, but here's where you can apply your project management skills. Break down your career goals into stages—where do you see yourself in one year, five years, or ten years? Use visual planning tools to map out these goals, along with the necessary steps and skills needed to get there. Regularly review and adjust your plans to match your growth and changing aspirations. Remember, flexibility is key—allow your plans to evolve as you gather more experience and insights about your strengths and passions.

By leveraging these strategies, you're not just navigating your career path—you're paving it with the unique bricks of your ADHD-enhanced skills. I know that this journey hasn't always been easy, and you've faced challenges that others might not understand. But your resilience and creativity are truly inspiring, and you should be proud of who you are and how far you've come. Whether it's turning your knack for organization into a showcased strength in reviews, structuring your networking efforts, seizing learning opportunities, or planning your career trajectory with a visually engaging and flexible plan, each step you take is a testament to transforming ADHD challenges into professional assets. So go ahead, harness these strategies, and watch as doors you might not even have noticed start opening up along your career path.

236 | EFFORTLESS ADHD ORGANIZATION

Chapter Checklist

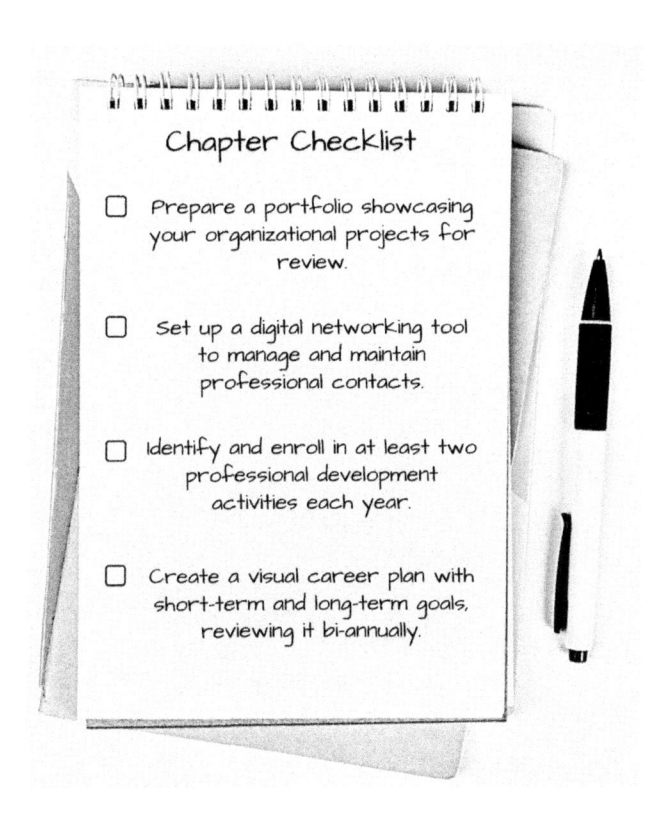

- ☐ Prepare a portfolio showcasing your organizational projects for review.

- ☐ Set up a digital networking tool to manage and maintain professional contacts.

- ☐ Identify and enroll in at least two professional development activities each year.

- ☐ Create a visual career plan with short-term and long-term goals, reviewing it bi-annually.

Bullet Point Summary

- Showcase your ADHD-driven organizational skills in performance reviews.
- Implement a structured, personalized approach to networking.
- Actively seek and engage in professional development opportunities.
- Use visual tools for long-term career planning, allowing for flexibility and growth.

PART VII

LIFESTYLE ORGANIZATION: FROM DAILY ROUTINES TO SPECIAL EVENTS

Imagine this: your home is filled with the remnants of half-started projects—paints from a night of artistic inspiration, fabric from a week when fashion design was your passion, and a guitar you swore you'd learn to play (but now it's just a very expensive coat rack). It sounds like the creative chaos of a typical ADHD mind, where hobbies breed faster than rabbits, and half the time, you forget where you put them. Don't worry; you're in good company, and this chapter is all about turning that creative chaos into an organized sanctuary where hobbies don't just start but actually flourish and, dare I say, finish.

CHAPTER 7.1

ORGANIZING PERSONAL PROJECTS AND HOBBIES

When it comes to personal projects and hobbies, your enthusiasm can often be as cluttered as your workspace. Each new interest sparks a flurry of activity—buying supplies, scouring the internet for tutorials, perhaps a late-night brainstorming session. But without a system, these projects can quickly become just another pile of 'stuff' in your creative space. Let's tackle this with some clever cataloging and organization.

Cataloging Projects and Supplies

First things first, let's talk cataloging. This isn't about creating a museum-worthy filing system but about stopping you from buying your fourth set of acrylic paints because you've lost the first three. Start by listing your ongoing projects and their necessary supplies. Use a simple spreadsheet or a dedicated app like Trello or Evernote, where you can update and track your stash in real-time. Photograph what you have, and tag these images with keywords so you can easily search for what you need. This digital catalog saves you time and money. It helps you deal with the frustration of misplaced items, allowing you more time to actually enjoy your hobbies.

Setting Up Dedicated Spaces

Now, onto crafting your creative haven. Dedicated spaces are crucial. They signal to your brain that it's "hobby time," helping shift gears from the daily grind to relaxation and creativity. And let's be honest, without a designated space, you're one "I'll put this here for now" away from losing your glue gun under a pile of random craft supplies. This space doesn't need to be large—a corner of a room or even a portable cart can serve as your personal studio. The key is consistency. Stock your hobby area with the necessary tools and make it visually appealing. A pegboard for tools, a small shelf for supplies, and good lighting can make a world of difference. It's about creating a space that invites you in rather than one that overwhelms you with chaos and half-finished projects.

Time Allocation for Hobbies

Balancing hobbies with life's myriad responsibilities is a common struggle, especially when your ADHD brain juggles multiple interests alongside family and career obligations. Here's a pro tip: integrate hobby time into your schedule as you would any necessary appointment. Whether it's a 30-minute session post-dinner or a couple of hours on a Sunday afternoon, write it down in your calendar. Treat this time as non-negotiable—you wouldn't skip a doctor's appointment because you're busy; give your hobby the same respect.

Project Completion Techniques

Starting projects is fun; finishing them—well, that's where things get tricky. It's like assembling IKEA furniture: you're excited at first, but by step 47, you're just wondering where all these extra screws came from. To see projects through to completion, break them into mini-tasks and set deadlines for each, creating a timeline that leads to the end goal. Celebrate milestones along the way—a finished chapter, a completed scarf, or a fully assembled model (extra screws optional). These celebrations reinforce your progress and motivate you to keep going. Think of it as giving high-fives to your future self, who will definitely appreciate not having to hunt for the scissors you misplaced three days ago.

By implementing these strategies, you not only make room for your hobbies in your schedule and space but also enhance your ability to enjoy and complete them. I know it can be challenging to juggle so many interests when life gets hectic, but remember that taking time for what you love is so important. You deserve a dedicated space and time to nurture your passions, and I'm so proud of you for making that a priority. Remember, organizing isn't just about tidiness—it's about making your environment work for you, enabling you to live fully in your passions and pursuits. Here's to not just starting but finishing your next great project—may it be as fulfilling as the process itself.

Time to turn this chaos into accomplishments!
PLANNER
Let's give everything a proper name and place!
FUTURE MASTER PIECE.
Sticky Situatio
Tangle Tamer
CREATIVITY IN OUR BLOOD
PAINT
PAI
A workspace that sparks joy!
Scheduling my hobbies like a pro!
PLANNER
creative HOUR
Crafting Session
Paint Party
Another project done—time to celebrate!
DONE!
COMPLETE
PLANNER
COMPLETE
From chaos to creativity—mission accomplished!
With humor and the right strategies, Hobby Harry turns hobby chaos into a series of rewarding accomplishments!

Chapter Checklist

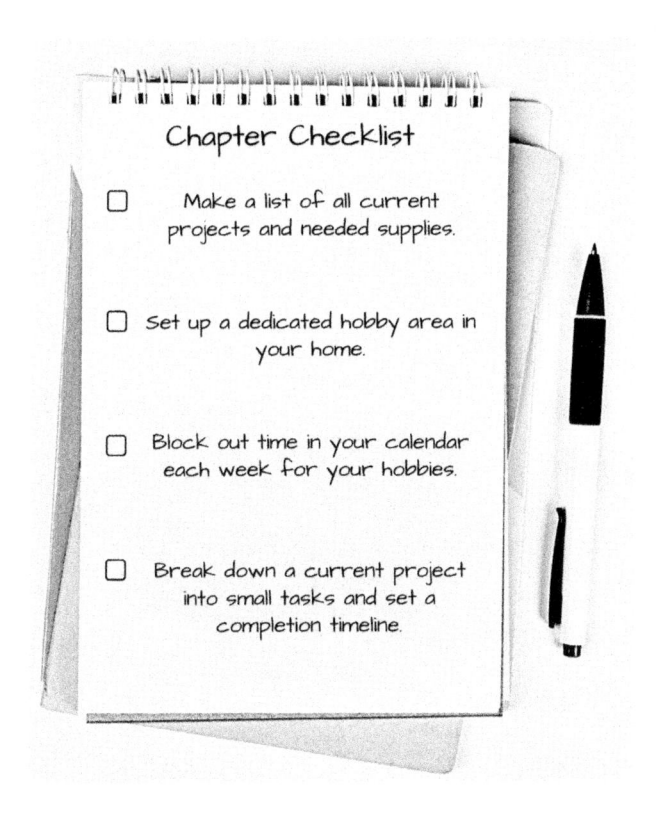

- ☐ Make a list of all current projects and needed supplies.

- ☐ Set up a dedicated hobby area in your home.

- ☐ Block out time in your calendar each week for your hobbies.

- ☐ Break down a current project into small tasks and set a completion timeline.

Bullet Point Summary

- Catalog ongoing projects and supplies digitally for easy tracking.
- Create a dedicated, inviting space for hobbies.
- Schedule regular, non-negotiable time slots for hobbies.
- Break projects into manageable tasks with set deadlines and celebrate milestones.

CHAPTER 7.2

STREAMLINING YOUR SOCIAL LIFE: EVENTS AND OUTINGS

Imagine you're the director of a blockbuster movie where every social event or outing is a major scene. Now, think of your digital calendar as the script—it guides the actors, sets the scenes, and ensures everyone knows their cues. Mastering this tool can turn even the most chaotic gatherings into award-winning performances. Start by integrating your social events into one comprehensive digital calendar. Platforms like Google Calendar or Outlook are fantastic because they let you color-code different types of events and set reminders. This isn't just about remembering when Aunt Sally's birthday party starts—it's about prepping for it without the last-minute panic.

Now, let's get to the nitty-gritty of pre-event planning, which can often feel like trying to solve a Rubik's cube blindfolded while someone throws more pieces at you. To avoid that chaos, develop a check-list for each event type you host or attend. And this isn't just any check-list; think of it as your event-planning bible. It should cover everything from dietary restrictions (because someone will always have a random one) and menu planning to venue arrangements and activity schedules. For a dinner party, your check-list might include confirming guest numbers, planning the menu (while mentally juggling food allergies), and setting up the dining area a day in advance. This proactive approach means you can enjoy the party instead of frantically Googling 'how to fix a burnt lasagna' an hour before guests arrive.

Delegation is your best friend, especially when your ADHD makes it tempting to either procrastinate or hyperfocus on things like color-coding the napkins while the main course is still frozen. For your next event, break down tasks and assign them to friends, family, or co-workers. This not only lightens your load but also makes others feel involved (and, let's face it, less likely to judge your playlist choices). For instance, assign someone the fun job of DJ to handle the music while someone else takes charge of capturing memories with photos. It's like being a conductor—except instead of violins, you've got your cousin managing snacks like a pro.

Post-event follow-up often gets neglected, but it's like the closing credits of your successful movie—they matter. Set up a system for thanking guests, which could be as simple as a WhatsApp message or a personalized thank you card. Also, consider a shared digital photo album where guests can upload and share memories from the event. Automate what you can; for instance, scheduling email thank-you notes to go out the day after the event ensures no one feels forgotten.

By embracing these strategies, you transform event planning and execution from a stress-inducing frenzy into a well-orchestrated, enjoyable experience. I know it can sometimes feel overwhelming juggling all the details, but you've shown incredible strength and creativity in making it all come together. Remember, it's okay to ask for help and lean on those who care about you—we're all here to support you. Whether it's a small family gathering or a significant corporate event, these tools empower you to handle it with grace and efficiency, leaving you not just with successful events but also with cherished memories and strengthened relationships.

250 | EFFORTLESS ADHD ORGANIZATION

Chapter Checklist

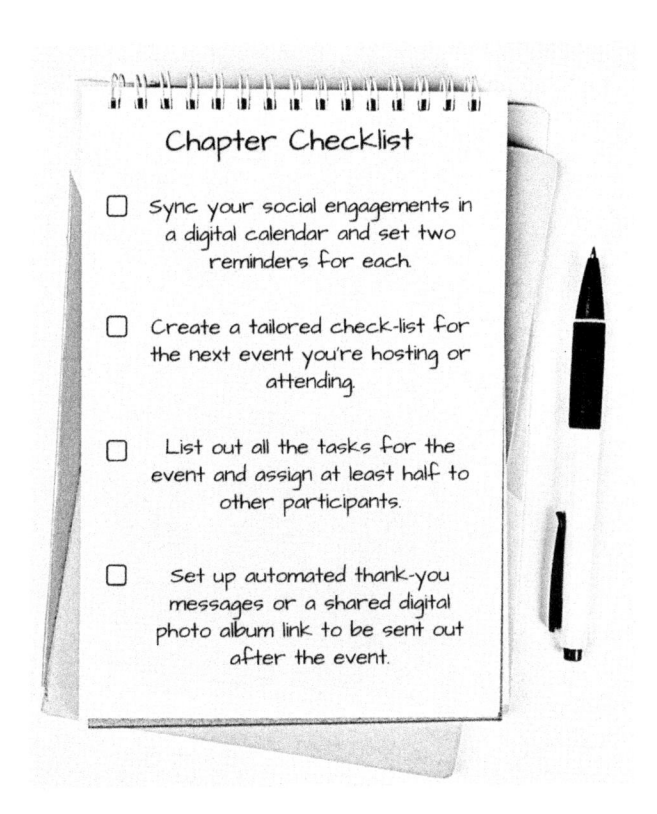

- ☐ Sync your social engagements in a digital calendar and set two reminders for each.

- ☐ Create a tailored check-list for the next event you're hosting or attending.

- ☐ List out all the tasks for the event and assign at least half to other participants.

- ☐ Set up automated thank-you messages or a shared digital photo album link to be sent out after the event.

Bullet Point Summary

- Integrate and manage social events using a digital calendar with reminders.
- Develop detailed check-lists for different types of events to ensure all aspects are covered.
- Delegate tasks to reduce workload and involve others in the event process.
- Automate post-event follow-up to maintain connections and express gratitude efficiently.

CHAPTER 7.3

TRAVEL MADE EASY: PACKING AND PLANNING TIPS

Ever found yourself frantically searching for your passport an hour before your flight, or realizing you packed five pairs of shoes but forgot underwear? Traveling can turn even the most organized individual into a headless chicken, especially when ADHD is in the mix, making the ability to focus and remember details akin to herding cats. But fear not, here's a game plan that transforms pre-trip chaos into a breezy departure, ensuring that your travel experience starts on a high note, not a frantic one.

Check-lists for Packing

The foundation of stress-free travel packing is a well-crafted check-list. Think of it as your packing playlist—every item has its beat, and missing one can throw off the whole rhythm. To tailor this to your life, create different check-lists for various travel scenarios: one for business trips, another for leisure vacations, and a third for family getaways. Each list should cater to the specifics of the occasion. For a business trip, your list might include not only clothing and toiletries but also tech gadgets, chargers, and perhaps presentation materials or samples. Leisure trips might call for swimwear, reading material, and maybe an adventurous spirit (though, sadly, that can't be packed!). Family trips? Well, that's a whole opera of needs, from snacks and entertainment to first aid and comfort items. Keep these lists saved in your favorite digital note-taking app. Before each trip, review and update the check-list to suit your current needs, which saves you from the dreaded "Oh no, I forgot the..." moment as you drive away from your house.

Itinerary Planning

Your itinerary is your travel symphony—the better it's composed, the more harmonious your trip. Start by outlining the broad strokes: travel dates, destinations, and accommodations. Then, like adding instruments to an orchestra, begin layering in the details: estimated travel times, key addresses, and planned activities. Because let's be honest, without the details, your symphony might end up sounding like a toddler with a drum set. Utilize travel planning tools like TripIt, which can consolidate all your travel confirmations—flights, hotels, rentals—into one streamlined itinerary accessible across your devices. This tool can sync with your calendar and share your plans with family or colleagues, ensuring everyone is on the same page. Remember, the goal here is clarity and accessibility. The more clearly each part of your trip is laid out, the less you'll scramble through emails for booking confirmations or wonder why you're at the airport a day early—again.

Essential Travel Apps

In the digital age, your smartphone is as crucial as your passport. Equip it with apps that smooth over potential travel wrinkles. For flight tracking and updates, consider apps like FlightAware, which keeps you informed about your flight status and even airport conditions. It's like having a personal assistant—minus the coffee runs. For on-the-ground logistics, Google Maps remains a traveler's best friend, offering not only directions but also restaurant reviews, so you don't accidentally end up at a place with one star and a questionable hygiene rating. And for those international adventures, don't forget a currency conversion app like XE Currency because no one wants to find themselves trying to mentally calculate exchange rates when they're just trying to buy a gelato without blowing their entire travel budget.

Unpacking and Re-organizing Post-Travel

Returning from travel can often feel like you've brought a piece of the chaos home with you. Suitcases linger, half-unpacked, clothes sprawled across the room. You tell yourself you'll unpack later, but three weeks pass, and you're still fishing socks out of your suitcase like it's your personal wardrobe vending machine. Turn this part of your journey into a closing ceremony. Start by unpacking everything within 24 hours of arriving home. Yes, everything. Sort your items into laundry, storage, and immediate use. Have a designated spot for travel-specific items like adapters or travel pillows so they're easy to find the next time. This swift unpacking process not only clears your physical space but also your mental space, allowing you to transition back to daily life seamlessly.

By integrating these strategies, travel becomes less about the stress of preparation and more about the joy of the experience. I know how overwhelming the details can feel, but I'm so proud of you for taking steps to make your journeys smoother and more enjoyable. With your digital tools in one hand and your well-crafted plans in the other, the world isn't just a place to visit—it's a place to enjoy. Remember, every adventure you embark on is a testament to your strength and willingness to embrace new experiences. You've got this!

Chapter Checklist

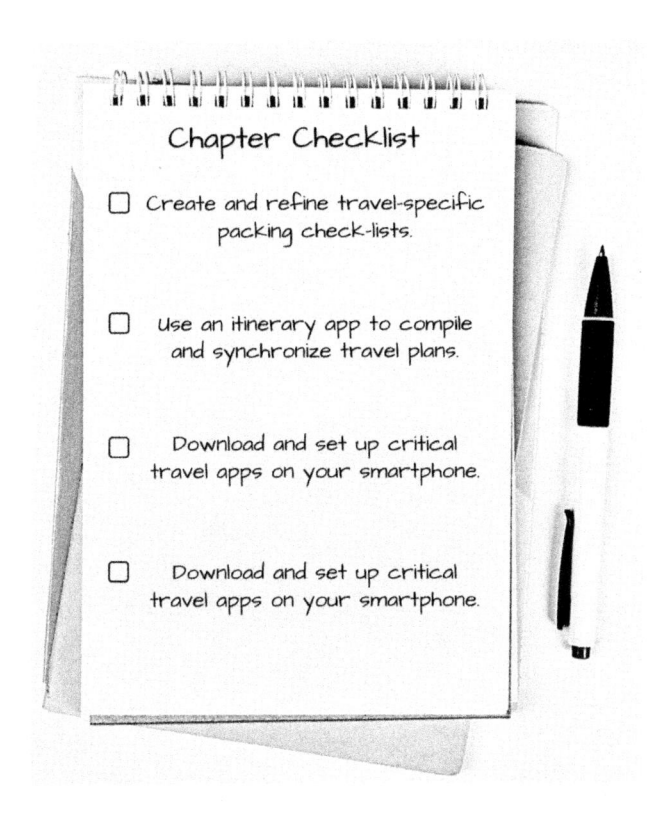

☐ Create and refine travel-specific packing check-lists.

☐ Use an itinerary app to compile and synchronize travel plans.

☐ Download and set up critical travel apps on your smartphone.

☐ Download and set up critical travel apps on your smartphone.

Bullet Point Summary

- Tailored packing check-lists for different types of travel.
- Detailed, accessible itineraries using synchronization tools.
- Essential travel apps for logistics, locations, and conversions.
- Efficient unpacking and re-organizing strategies post-travel.

CHAPTER 7.4

BALANCING SOCIAL AND PERSONAL TIME EFFECTIVELY

Striking the perfect balance between your social engagements and cherished personal downtime can sometimes feel like trying to stand on a seesaw—just when you think you've got it balanced, life throws another event your way--now your butt is confused and in the dirt. As someone managing ADHD, you might find this balancing act particularly challenging. Your vibrant, outgoing side wants to say yes to every gathering and every coffee date. Still, there's also a part of you that craves quiet, structured time at home to recharge and indulge in your hobbies. Let's navigate this tightrope together with some practical strategies, ensuring that you maintain your social butterfly status while also honoring your need for personal retreats.

Prioritizing Personal Time

It's crucial, and yes, absolutely necessary, to carve out time for yourself. This isn't selfish—it's self-care. Communicating this need to friends and family is key, and it can be done without sounding like a hermit. When you're planning your week, consciously block out periods for 'me-time.' Whether it's reading, painting, or simply binge-watching your favorite series, make these blocks non-negotiable. Explain to your loved ones why this time is important—a well-rested, mentally refreshed you is much more fun at parties anyway. Use phrases like, "I'm spending some time to recharge tonight so I can be fully there at brunch tomorrow!" It shows that you're not just avoiding social interactions but are managing your energy wisely.

Integrating Social and Personal Calendars

Now for the jigsaw puzzle of integrating your social and personal calendars. Visual tools are your best friend here—after all, if it's not color-coded, did you even plan it? Use a digital calendar that allows color coding—maybe blue for personal activities and green for social events. Seeing your week laid out visually helps you immediately spot if you're overbooking socially or, worse, accidentally planning "me time" that turns into Netflix and a nap marathon. Apps like Google Calendar or Outlook offer features where you can overlay multiple calendars to get a holistic view of your commitments. This integration acts as a preventative measure against the all-too-common double-booking, or worse, the dreaded no-booking where you end up overwhelmed or wondering why your social life suddenly feels like a ghost town.

Saying No Gracefully

Learning to say no is an art, especially when your natural inclination is to say yes to avoid disappointing anyone. Here's a gentle way to decline: acknowledge the invite, express your appreciation, and be honest about why you can't attend. Something like, "Thank you so much for thinking of me! I've promised myself some downtime this weekend to recharge. Let's definitely catch up next week, though!" This approach is honest, respectful, and keeps the door open for future interactions. Remember, saying no doesn't close down social opportunities—it just postpones them to a time when you can fully enjoy them.

Recharge Strategies

For those times when social interactions take a toll, and you find yourself drained, having quick recharge strategies up your sleeve is essential. Consider short, meditative breathing exercises—which can be done almost anywhere. Even a five-minute session can significantly boost your mental energy. Think of it like restarting your computer when it's acting glitchy, except, you know, you won't lose all your open tabs (hopefully). For a physical recharge, a brief walk, preferably in nature, can do wonders. These activities act like a system reboot, giving you that much-needed pause and refresh—without the dreaded "spinning color wheel of death" moment!

Navigating the delicate balance of social and personal time doesn't have to feel like a high-wire act. I know it can be challenging when your vibrant energy pulls you toward social events, but your mind craves that peaceful downtime. Remember, it's perfectly okay to prioritize yourself—you're not letting anyone down by taking care of your own needs. With these strategies, you can enjoy the best of both worlds, keeping your social life vibrant while respecting your personal boundaries and needs for downtime. Whether you're tuning in to your favorite show or toasting with friends, balance is key—not just in what you do, but in how you recharge and reflect afterward. You've got this, and I'm here cheering you on every step of the way!

How did everything turn into a party?
Rain check, please!
INVITATION
RAIN CHECK
I need to fix this before I burn out!
Let's get this right!
work
relaxation
personal time
Not this time, but soon!
RAIN CHECK
INVITATION
Balance restored, and I'm ready for anything!
With humor and a bit of magic, Social Sam navigates his week, finding the perfect balance between social events and personal time!

Chapter Checklist

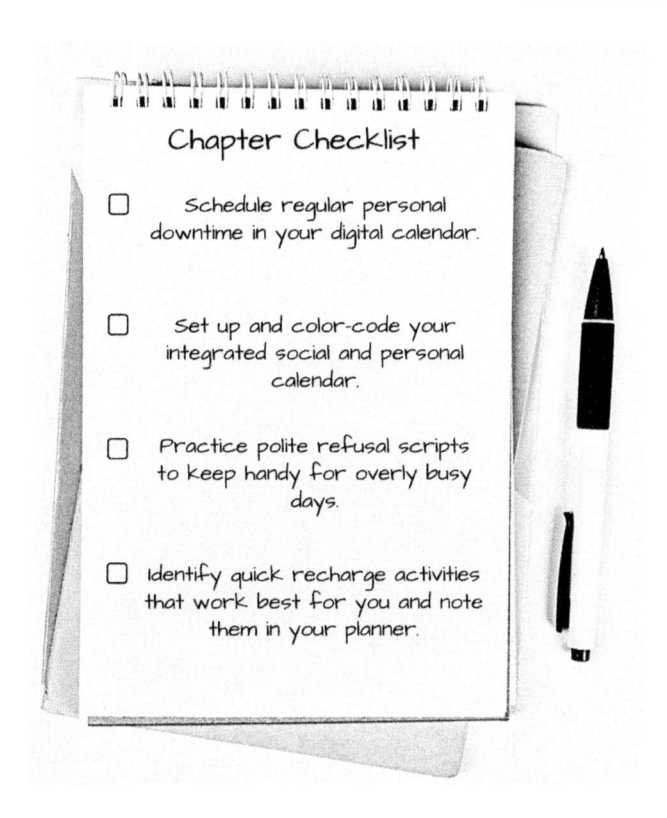

- ☐ Schedule regular personal downtime in your digital calendar.
- ☐ Set up and color-code your integrated social and personal calendar.
- ☐ Practice polite refusal scripts to keep handy for overly busy days.
- ☐ Identify quick recharge activities that work best for you and note them in your planner.

Bullet Point Summary

- Block out non-negotiable personal time each week.
- Integrate and color-code personal and social calendars for visual management.
- Decline invitations gracefully with honest and respectful communication.
- Employ quick, effective strategies for recharging after draining social interactions.

CHAPTER 7.5

SEASONAL ORGANIZING: ADJUSTING YOUR SPACE AND SCHEDULE

As the leaves change color and you find yourself swapping flip-flops for fuzzy socks, it's a clear signal—just like your favorite latte turning pumpkin-spiced—that it's time to shift gears in your home and routine. Seasonal changes aren't just about enjoying new weather; they're about aligning your life with the rhythm of the world outside your window. This can be a delightful process if you manage it with the same creativity and flair you apply to selecting your autumn playlist or your spring cleaning tunes. Here, we'll navigate the art of seasonal decluttering, adjusting routines, and finding smart storage for those seasonal items that seem to crawl from the woodwork every few months.

Seasonal Decluttering Routines

As seasons shift, so do our activities and the items we use daily. This transition period is the perfect time for what I like to call 'seasonal decluttering.' It's like matchmaking your belongings with the season—ensuring that only those truly in love with the current weather stick around in your immediate space. Begin by pulling out all the items distinctly tied to the past season. Yes, that includes the inflatable pool, which is now sadly deflated in the corner. Assess each item's fate based on its use, condition, and the joy it brought you during its tenure. If it's still a heartwarmer, it stays (but more on where it remains in a moment). Everything else? Thank them for their service with a Marie Kondo-esque nod and find them a new home, be it via donation, selling, or recycling.

Adjusting Routines for Seasons

Your daily routine needs a seasonal shake-up just as much as your wardrobe does—because, let's be honest, no one wants to be stuck in winter mode when summer calls for flip-flops and ice cream. It keeps your activities fresh and aligned with natural energy levels influenced by changes in daylight and weather. For instance, if you're a runner, summer might mean early morning jogs to avoid the heat. At the same time, autumn could see you enjoying evening runs in the crisp air—unless, of course, you get distracted by the smell of pumpkin spice everywhere. Apply this adaptive thinking to your eating habits, too—summer might be all about smoothies and salads, but come winter, your soul (and body) will thank you for hearty soups and warm bread. This shift not only keeps your routine in harmony with the season but also keeps you engaged and less likely to fall into a rut.

Seasonal Storage Solutions

Now, back to storing those beloved seasonal items. Practical storage solutions will save you from the all-too-familiar chaos of seasonal item avalanches every time you open that closet—because nothing says "Good morning!" like being attacked by a rogue winter boot in July. First, identify storage spaces in your home ideally suited for out-of-season items—under the bed, high shelves in closets, or even a section of your garage. Use clear, labeled bins for physical transparency and mental peace—because, let's face it, rummaging through six boxes labeled "miscellaneous" is a surefire way to lose an entire afternoon. For bulky items like winter coats or summer camping gear, consider vacuum-sealed bags that not only save space but also protect your items from dust, moisture, and the odd spider looking for a new home.

Preparing for Seasonal Changes

Preparation is your secret weapon in the battle against seasonal chaos. Create a check-list for each season's onset, tailored to your personal and home needs. This check-list should cover everything from swapping out your wardrobe and checking the functionality of your heating system (nobody wants a cold surprise come first frost) to preparing your car for winter roads or updating your emergency kit—because yes, sometimes seasons bring surprises like blizzards or heat waves. Having this check-list not only keeps you one step ahead but also reduces the anxiety that can come with seasonal shifts.

By embracing these seasonal adjustments, you transform what could be a dreaded upheaval into an opportunity for renewal and order. I know it can be challenging to adapt to the constant changes each season brings, but you've shown such resilience and creativity in making it work. Each season brings its own charm and challenges, and you're more than ready to handle them with grace and style. With your newly streamlined approach, you're ready to meet them head-on, wrapped in the perfect scarf or sunhat, depending on the month. Remember, you're not just adjusting to the seasons—you're thriving in them, and I'm so proud of you for that.

Come on, just fit already!
BOING!
There's got to be a better way...
Prepare to be vacuum-sealed!
Who's the boss now?
Winter ready and summer sorted!
Seasonal Storage
With a bit of humor and the right tools, Seasonal Sue turns storage chaos into organized bliss!

Chapter Checklist

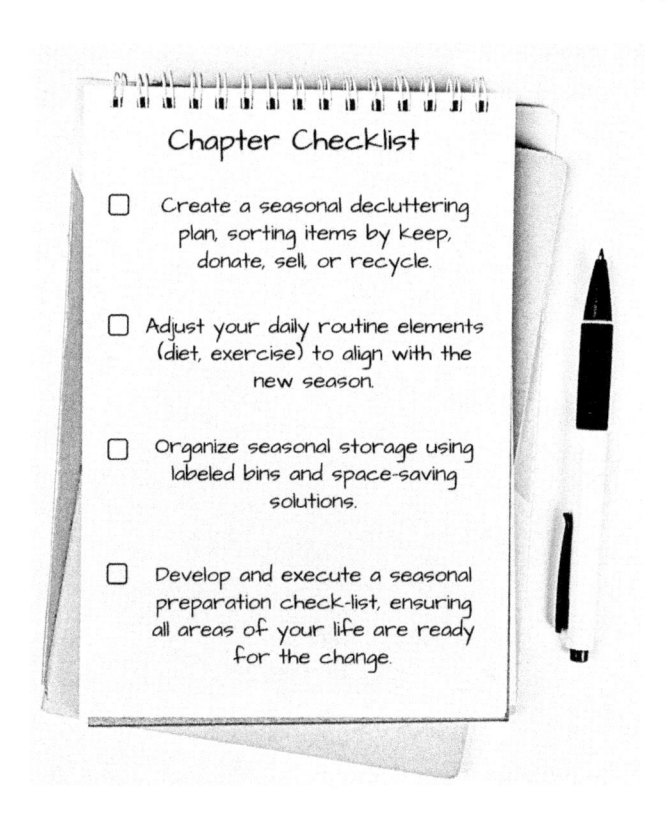

☐ Create a seasonal decluttering plan, sorting items by keep, donate, sell, or recycle.

☐ Adjust your daily routine elements (diet, exercise) to align with the new season.

☐ Organize seasonal storage using labeled bins and space-saving solutions.

☐ Develop and execute a seasonal preparation check-list, ensuring all areas of your life are ready for the change.

Bullet Point Summary

- Tackle seasonal decluttering by sorting and deciding the fate of out-of-season items.
- Adapt daily routines to match seasonal changes for freshness and energy alignment.
- Employ clear, labeled bins and vacuum-sealed bags for efficient off-season storage.
- Prepare for each season with a comprehensive check-list covering home, personal, and vehicle needs.

CHAPTER 7.6

MAINTAINING A MINIMALIST LIFESTYLE WITH ADHD

Imagine your space as a canvas where every item is a stroke of paint. Too many strokes, and you lose the picture in the chaos. Trust me, I've tried adding every color at once—it ends up looking like a toddler's finger painting! Actually, I apologize: that was an insult to toddlers and their paintings everywhere! This is where minimalism steps in—a lifestyle choice that paints a serene picture by using only what's necessary. For those juggling the vibrant palette of ADHD, minimalism isn't just about aesthetics; it's a functional strategy that reduces the clutter that often clouds our minds and overwhelms our senses. It simplifies decision-making and cuts down the distractions that can make ADHD management feel like navigating a storm without a compass.

Benefits of Minimalism for ADHD

The minimalist approach offers a breath of fresh air if your mental space often feels as cluttered as a teenager's bedroom after a clothes-finding frenzy. By reducing the number of stimuli around you, you're not just clearing your physical space but also easing the cognitive load on your brain. Fewer choices mean less decision fatigue. Imagine your morning routine with a wardrobe that contains only the clothes you love and wear—suddenly, getting dressed is no longer a battle but a peaceful ritual. This simplicity can help enhance your focus and decrease the anxiety that often accompanies the chaos of too many options.

Steps to Adopt Minimalism

Transitioning to a minimalist lifestyle doesn't happen overnight—if it did, I'd probably lose my keys somewhere in the process. It's more about intentionality than austerity. Start by assessing what you truly need. Go through your belongings and ask yourself, 'Does this add value or joy to my life?'—and no, keeping a drawer full of random cords 'just in case' doesn't count. Begin with one room, perhaps the one that causes the most stress. Sort items into categories: keep, donate, sell, or throw away. Be honest but also patient with yourself—it's okay if you're not ready to part with certain things yet. Then, move on to digital decluttering. Unsubscribe from unused newsletters, delete old files and organize the rest into clearly labeled folders. It's like giving your brain a much-needed break from the chaos without the hassle of losing everything you own.

Maintaining Minimalism

Once you've set the foundations of your minimalist space, the challenge is to keep it that way. Implement a one-in, one-out policy—every time a new item comes into your home, one must leave. This rule helps maintain the balance without accumulating new clutter. Regularly revisit the goals of your minimalist lifestyle. Why did you choose this path? Reminding yourself of these reasons can renew your commitment when old habits threaten to resurface. Perhaps schedule a monthly review of your space and systems, adjusting as necessary to fit your current life circumstances and goals.

Overcoming Challenges in Minimalism

It's not all smooth sailing—sometimes it's more like trying to sail a boat while clinging to an old hoodie that 'might come back in style one day.' Emotional attachments to items or the pressure to conform to consumerist norms can derail your minimalist journey faster than a flash sale on Amazon. When you find it hard to let go of sentimental items, consider their true cost to your peace of mind and space. Sometimes, taking a photo can help preserve the memory without keeping the actual thing (because, let's be real, you don't need that mug from your cousin's wedding in 2004). As for societal pressure, focus on the benefits you've experienced—less stress, more clarity, and maybe even some extra cash from not buying things you didn't need. Those personal wins make it easier to resist the pull of mindless accumulation.

By embracing these strategies, you transform minimalism from a mere design aesthetic into a functional lifestyle choice that supports your ADHD management. I know it hasn't been easy to let go of certain items or to resist the pull of accumulating more, but you're making incredible strides toward creating a space that truly serves you. Remember, every small step you take is a victory worth celebrating. It's about crafting a living space and a lifestyle that brings tranquility, focus, and joy—quite the masterpiece on your life's canvas. You've got this!

274 | EFFORTLESS ADHD ORGANIZATION

Chapter Checklist

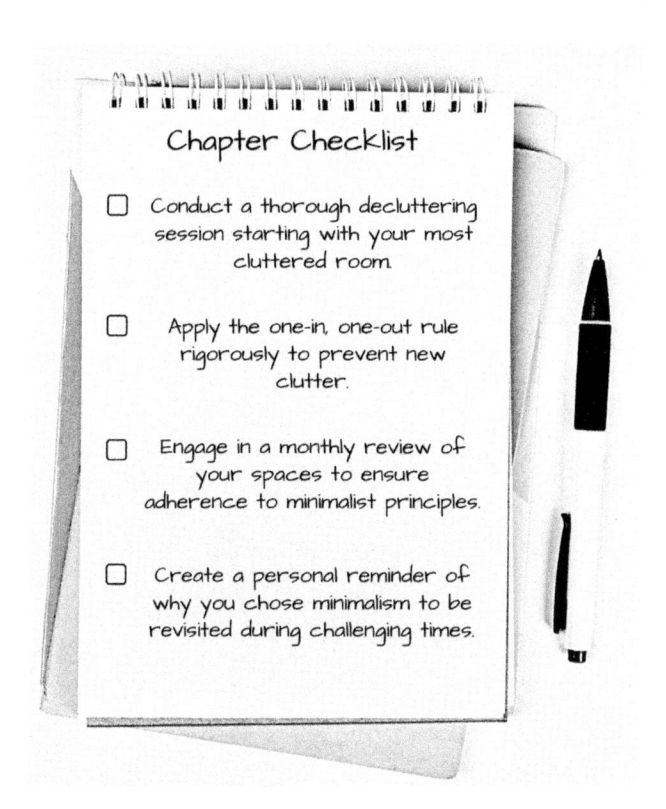

- ☐ Conduct a thorough decluttering session starting with your most cluttered room.

- ☐ Apply the one-in, one-out rule rigorously to prevent new clutter.

- ☐ Engage in a monthly review of your spaces to ensure adherence to minimalist principles.

- ☐ Create a personal reminder of why you chose minimalism to be revisited during challenging times.

Bullet Point Summary

- Minimalism reduces distractions and simplifies decision-making, which is beneficial for ADHD management.
- Start by assessing personal items for their value and joy, then declutter room by room.
- Maintain minimalism with a one-in, one-out policy and regular reviews of your minimalist goals.
- Tackle emotional attachments and societal pressures by focusing on the personal benefits of a simpler lifestyle.

PART VIII

ADVANCED ORGANIZING CHALLENGES AND SOLUTIONS

Imagine you're embarking on a road trip across the country. You've got snacks packed, playlists ready, and a car full of enthusiasm. But here's the twist: your map is a sprawling scroll that keeps rolling out the window, catching in the door, and generally making it impossible to see where you're headed next. That's a bit of what tackling long-term projects feels like when you have ADHD. Exciting, yes, but without the right strategies, it can turn into an overwhelming journey where you feel like you're constantly trying to catch the map. This chapter is about turning that unwieldy map into a GPS that not only shows you the way but also cheers you on as you go.

CHAPTER 8.1

LONG-TERM PROJECTS: STAYING ORGANIZED FROM START TO FINISH

Long-term projects are like marathons for the ADHD mind, which might prefer a series of sprints instead. You see the finish line way off in the distance, and it's all too easy to get distracted by a more attractive, immediate task—like rearranging your sock drawer or deep-diving into an internet rabbit hole about the history of cheese. To combat this, breaking down your mega project into manageable milestones and tasks is crucial. Visual planning tools like Gantt charts or project management software such as Asana can be your best allies here. They allow you to see a clear timeline and break down the project into smaller, less daunting pieces. Each task becomes a mini-goal, approachable, and achievable.

Imagine this scenario: you're writing a book (hey, maybe about organizing life with ADHD!). Instead of staring down the terrifying task of "write a book," you break it down: outline a chapter, research a topic, write 500 words, and so on. Each completed task is a step toward that bigger goal, and with each step, your confidence grows.

However, the plot thickens with the ADHD brain's love for novelty wearing off quickly. This is where regular review and adjustment come into play. Set bi-weekly or monthly check-ins on your project's progress. During these reviews, adjust your timelines and methods as needed. Maybe you've found that writing in short bursts is more productive than one long session. Or perhaps you need to switch up the order of your chapters because one section has unexpectedly inspired a brilliant new angle. These regular check-ins keep the project dynamic and responsive to your needs, rather than you having to stick to a rigid plan that doesn't work.

And what about those times when motivation wanes, or distractions multiply? This is when strategically placed reminders and alerts show their worth. Setting up notifications to keep you on track or scheduling specific times to work on your project can help fend off procrastination. It's like having a coach who knows exactly when you're likely to veer off track and shows up with exactly the right words of encouragement or a gentle nudge back on the path.

Let's remember the power of celebrating milestones. Completing each phase of your project deserves a mini-celebration—whether it's treating yourself to a movie night or just doing a happy dance in your living room (bonus points if you don't trip over that pile of laundry still waiting to be folded). Acknowledging your progress is crucial; it not only boosts your morale but also reinforces your belief in your ability to see things through—because who doesn't deserve a victory lap after finally finishing that "quick" 6-month project?

By approaching long-term projects with these strategies, you transform what could be an overwhelming trek into a series of enjoyable excursions. It's like turning a marathon into a fun run—with occasional dance breaks when your favorite song comes on!

Each step is planned, each milestone celebrated, and every adjustment a testament to your growing skill in managing not just projects but the winding roads of ADHD. Remember, it's okay to take things one step at a time, and it's perfectly fine if the path isn't always straight. You've shown extraordinary determination in breaking down big tasks into achievable pieces. Your ability to adapt and keep moving forward is truly inspiring. Keep up the great work—you've got this, and we're all cheering you on!

282 | EFFORTLESS ADHD ORGANIZATION

Let's get this project started!

Hey, give those back!

Gotcha! Now back to work.

I've never seen so much coffee in my life!

Here, this planner will help you stay on track.

I can build bridges to help you cross any obstacles.

Project completed! Thanks, everyone!

With humor and determination, Project Pat navigates the jungle of long-term projects, turning obstacles into opportunities!

Chapter Checklist

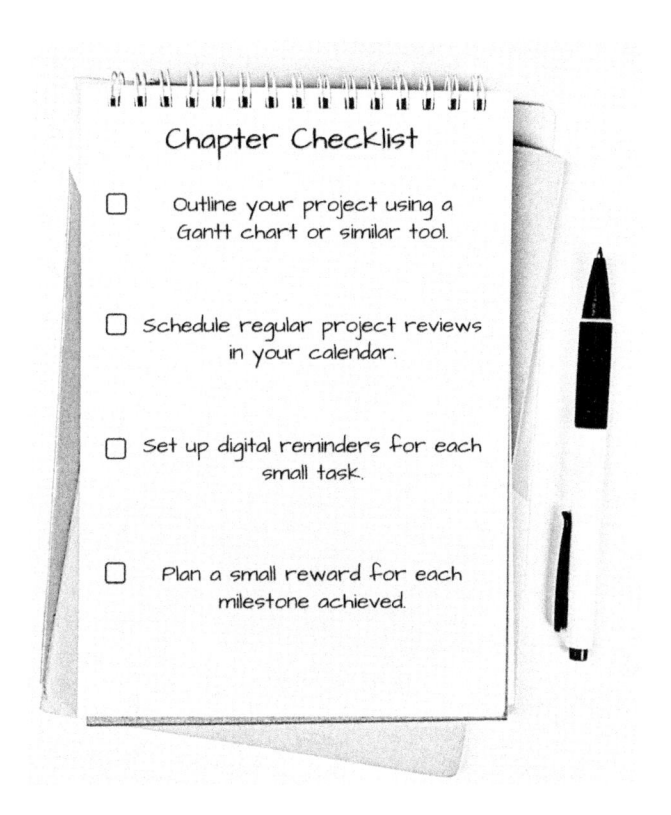

- ☐ Outline your project using a Gantt chart or similar tool.
- ☐ Schedule regular project reviews in your calendar.
- ☐ Set up digital reminders for each small task.
- ☐ Plan a small reward for each milestone achieved.

Bullet Point Summary

- Break projects into manageable tasks using visual tools.
- Regularly review and adjust project plans.
- Use reminders to maintain focus.
- Celebrate completed milestones to boost motivation.

CHAPTER 8.2

ORGANIZING FINANCIAL DOCUMENTS ADHD-FRIENDLY

Navigating the labyrinth of financial paperwork can feel a lot like trying to solve a Rubik's cube while riding a unicycle. For those of us blessed with ADHD, it's not just about keeping track of bills and receipts; it's about finding a system that doesn't make our brains want to go on a vacation. That's why a simplified, fool-proof filing system is more than a convenience—it's a necessity. Picture this: a filing system where every type of document has a home, and you don't have to sift through a mountain of paper to find your last electricity bill. Using clear, straightforward categories like 'Utilities,' 'Healthcare,' 'Taxes,' and 'Insurance,' each with its designated storage space, whether it's a physical folder or a digital directory, can turn hours of frantic searching into mere seconds.

Now, let's talk digital, shall we? In this gloriously digital age, apps and tools designed specifically for organizing financial documents can be a game-changer. Imagine an app that not only stores your documents but also categorizes them automatically as you upload. Tools like Mint or Quicken take the guesswork out of financial organization by automatically sorting your expenses into categories and even setting reminders for upcoming bills. This feature is particularly handy for those ADHD moments when 'pay the electric bill' competes with a thousand other thoughts for attention in your brain. These apps ensure that even if 'pay the bill' loses the battle one day, you're still covered. Plus, the less time you spend managing bills and statements, the more time you have for more enjoyable activities, like mastering the art of making the perfect pancake on a Sunday morning.

But what about the regular check-ups? Just like you need to visit the dentist to prevent cavities (because, let's face it, no one wants a surprise root canal), regular reviews of your financial documents can prevent fiscal headaches. Setting aside a specific time each month to go through your finances aligns this task with other routine activities like budgeting or preparing for tax season. It's about creating a rhythm that your ADHD brain can dance to—because, let's be honest, without a set rhythm, it's more like freestyle chaos! During these sessions, you can adjust budgets, ensure bills are paid, and even plan for future expenses. It's like taking a moment to tune your guitar before you play, ensuring that everything is in perfect harmony for the performance ahead.

Securing sensitive information, both physically and digitally, is akin to locking your treasure chest—except instead of pirates, you're protecting it from hackers and the occasional "Where did I put that?" moment. In the world of online banking and digital transactions, protecting your financial data is critical. Simple steps like using strong, unique passwords (yes, no more 'password123'), enabling two-factor authentication, and using a dedicated email address for financial communications can significantly enhance security. On the physical front, keeping important documents in a locked file cabinet and being mindful of what you carry in your wallet can prevent sensitive information from falling into the wrong hands. Think of it as setting booby traps around your treasure; only those with the right keys—or at least a sharp memory—can access the riches within.

By transforming your approach to organizing financial documents from a tangled mess to a streamlined process, you can not only save time but also avoid the stress and anxiety that come with financial disorganization. I know managing finances can feel overwhelming, especially when juggling the challenges of ADHD, but you're taking incredible steps toward making it easier on yourself. Remember, every slight improvement is a victory worth celebrating. With these strategies in place, you can focus more on the joys of life and less on where you placed that utility bill. You've got this, and I'm proud of you for taking control of your financial well-being!

S.S. Finance
Where did all these receipts come from?!
I need to get these under control!
Time to go digital!
Almost there!
S.S. Finance
Chaos conquered!
Smooth sailing from here on out!
Financial Freedom AHEAD!
With a bit of humor and the right tools, Finance Fred turns the wild seas of financial chaos into smooth sailing!

Chapter Checklist

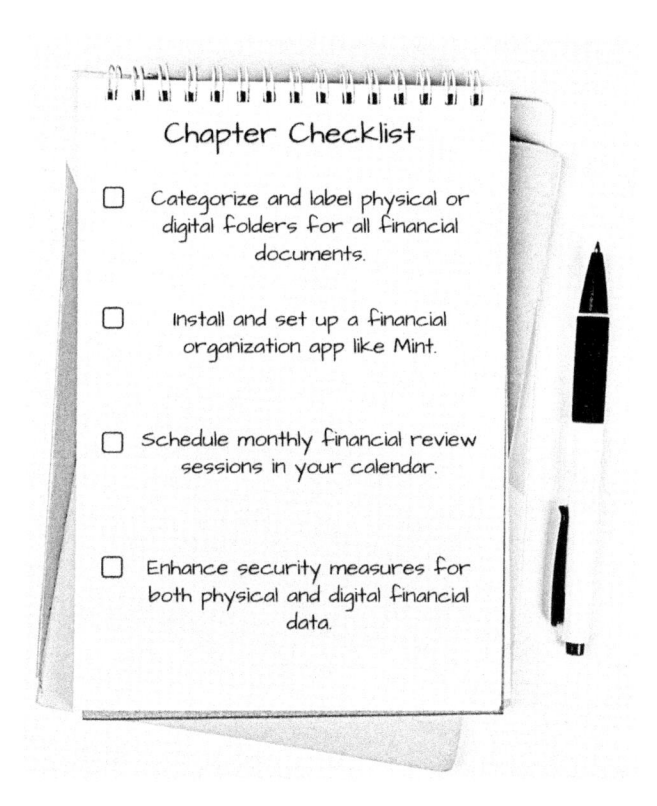

- ☐ Categorize and label physical or digital folders for all financial documents.

- ☐ Install and set up a financial organization app like Mint.

- ☐ Schedule monthly financial review sessions in your calendar.

- ☐ Enhance security measures for both physical and digital financial data.

Bullet Point Summary

- Implement a simple, categorized filing system for financial documents.
- Utilize digital tools for automatic categorization and reminders.
- Conduct regular financial reviews to keep everything in check.
- Secure sensitive information to protect against fraud and theft.

CHAPTER 8.3

OVERCOMING THE CHALLENGES OF HYPERFOCUS IN ORGANIZATION

Have you ever found yourself so absorbed in a task that the world around you seems to disappear? That's hyperfocus. It's like your brain has its own superzoom lens, and when it locks on, everything else blurs. It's also like a moth flying towards a "beautiful" bug zapper "Must. Touch. The Light"! This intense concentration can be a superpower when harnessed correctly, but let's look it in the eyes; it can also turn into a sneaky villain, hijacking your time and focus from other pressing tasks. So, how do you keep this powerful beast on a leash? Let's unpack some strategies to balance hyperfocus with the flexibility your life demands.

Balancing focus with flexibility is akin to being a DJ at a party. You have to read the room (your tasks), know when to ramp up the beat (intensify focus), and recognize when it's time to mellow out (shift focus). This balance prevents you from spending three hours perfecting a single graphic for a presentation while the rest of your tasks pile up like unread emails. To achieve this, start by clearly defining the scope and goals of each task before you dive in. It's like setting up bumpers in bowling; they keep you aligned and prevent you from veering into the gutter of endless perfectionism.

Setting strict time boundaries is your next best move. Think of it as setting up a playpen for your focus—because, let's be real, without it, your brain will wander off like a toddler in a toy store. Use timers—yes, those lovely devices that ding when time's up—to remind you when to start and stop a task. This helps prevent you from disappearing down a research rabbit hole and resurfacing three hours later, knowing way too much about penguin migration patterns. For example, if you need to research for a report, set a timer for 30 minutes. Once it rings, it's your cue to review what you've gathered and decide if you genuinely need more time or if it's time to move on. This way, hyperfocus becomes a timed event, not an all-day marathon.

Now, let's talk about channeling your hyperfocus productively. It's about making this trait a tool rather than a hindrance. Start by directing your hyperfocus toward complex or less appealing tasks that require a deep dive. This approach turns a potential drawback into your secret weapon. Say you dread data analysis, a task awaiting you at work. By aligning your hyperfocus with this task, you transform what is usually a tedious process into a challenge you're equipped to tackle head-on. Before you know it, you're finding patterns and insights like a pro because your hyperfocus has turned the task into a puzzle your brain is itching to solve.

Incorporating mindfulness techniques can also greatly enhance your ability to manage hyperfocus. Mindfulness teaches you to observe your mental state and recognize the signs of hyperfocus setting in. It's like having a mental surveillance system; it alerts you when hyperfocus tries to sneak past your mental security. Simple practices like mindful breathing or quick meditative pauses help recalibrate your attention. They allow you to step back, assess if your current focus aligns with your priorities, and make adjustments as needed. It's not about stopping hyperfocus but guiding it wisely. Hyperfocus isn't unlike a 5-year-old...capable of both making a big stink if left unattended in the corner and creating colorfully satisfying works of finger-paint if guided and left with the right tools.

By reining in hyperfocus and using it to your advantage, you not only optimize your productivity but also turn what could be a disruptive trait into one of your strongest assets. I know it can be challenging to balance that intense focus with the flexibility life often requires, but your effort to harness it is truly inspiring. Remember, it's okay to take breaks and adjust your focus when needed—you're doing a fantastic job navigating this journey. Keep believing in yourself because your ability to channel your hyperfocus is a powerful tool that sets you apart. Whether it's powering through a detailed project, conquering mundane tasks, or simply managing your day-to-day responsibilities, understanding and controlling your hyperfocus lets you navigate your tasks with precision and agility.

294 | EFFORTLESS ADHD ORGANIZATION

Chapter Checklist

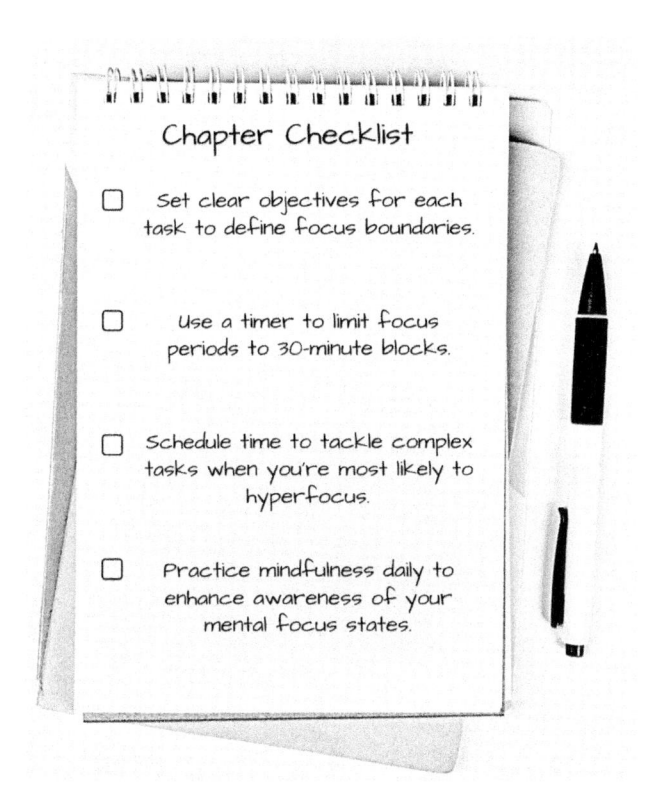

- ☐ Set clear objectives for each task to define focus boundaries.
- ☐ Use a timer to limit focus periods to 30-minute blocks.
- ☐ Schedule time to tackle complex tasks when you're most likely to hyperfocus.
- ☐ Practice mindfulness daily to enhance awareness of your mental focus states.

Bullet Point Summary

- Balance intense focus with flexibility to manage various tasks effectively.
- Use timers to set boundaries for periods of deep concentration.
- Direct hyperfocus towards complex or challenging tasks.
- Employ mindfulness to monitor and adjust the level of focus.

CHAPTER 8.4

ADVANCED LABELING AND SORTING TECHNIQUES

Let's face it, the word 'organizing' can sometimes send shivers down the spine of anyone with ADHD, conjuring up images of endless bins and labels that just don't stick — figuratively and literally. But what if I told you that there's a way to make this not just manageable but actually enjoyable? Yes, with some clever tricks up your sleeve, you can transform your cluttered chaos into an ordered oasis that even your non-ADHD friends might envy. Let's dive into the colorful world of advanced labeling and sorting techniques designed to cater specifically to the visual processing preferences that many of us with ADHD share.

Picture this: every item in your workspace or home has a color tag, creating a rainbow of functionality. This isn't just about making things look pretty (though that's a definite plus); it's about utilizing color coding and visual tags to tap directly into the ADHD brain's inherent love for vivid, stimulating visuals. For instance, imagine your filing system where all financial documents are tagged in green (think money!), medical records in red (urgent!), and personal letters in blue (calm skies ahead!). This method isn't just aesthetically pleasing; it reduces the time you spend hunting for documents and increases the time you can spend doing... well, anything else!

But why stop at manual tagging? In the digital age, electronic labeling systems are like the superheroes of organization—if Superman also had a label maker. These aren't your average label makers, either. We're talking about sophisticated systems that not only label but also categorize and update your files with just a click. Tools like Evernote or Microsoft OneNote can be your digital librarians, keeping your electronic files in impeccable order. They allow you to tag each file or note with keywords that you can search later, making retrieval a breeze. And the best part? They sync across all your devices, so whether you're on your phone, tablet, or computer, your files are organized just how your ADHD brain always dreamed—without the chaos.

Now, let's tackle the beast of multi-layered sorting systems. For those of us with ADHD, our collections of items or information often snowball and can get overwhelming. That's where advanced sorting systems come into play. Imagine a system that not only organizes your books alphabetically but also by genre, then by author, and even the color of the spine. This might sound over the top, but for the ADHD mind, this level of categorization can make the difference between a frustrating search and an enjoyable retrieval experience. Whether it's hierarchical (breaking down categories into subcategories), alphabetical, or thematic, the key is to build a system that feels intuitive to you.

But what about keeping these systems in check? Just like a garden, our organizational systems need regular tending to thrive—and let's be honest, if your plants can't survive without water for three months, your files probably can't either. This is where review and reorganization cycles become essential. Every few months, take a day to go through your organized spaces and digital systems to make sure everything still makes sense. Is your blue tag for personal items still relevant, or has it become a junk drawer in disguise? Are your digital files still syncing correctly across all devices, or are they playing hide and seek with you? This regular maintenance ensures that your systems evolve along with your changing needs, keeping them both effective and (mostly) stress-free.

By embracing these advanced techniques, you turn the mundane task of organizing into a vibrant and visually stimulating activity that not only appeals to your creative inclinations but also significantly enhances your productivity and reduces stress. I know it might feel overwhelming at first, but remember that every small step you take is a victory worth celebrating. You're not just organizing your space; you're creating an environment that reflects your unique brilliance and supports your journey. So, grab those labels, fire up your digital organizers, and transform your space into a model of ADHD-friendly efficiency that even the most organized minds would admire. You've got this, and I'm cheering you on every step of the way!

300 | EFFORTLESS ADHD ORGANIZATION

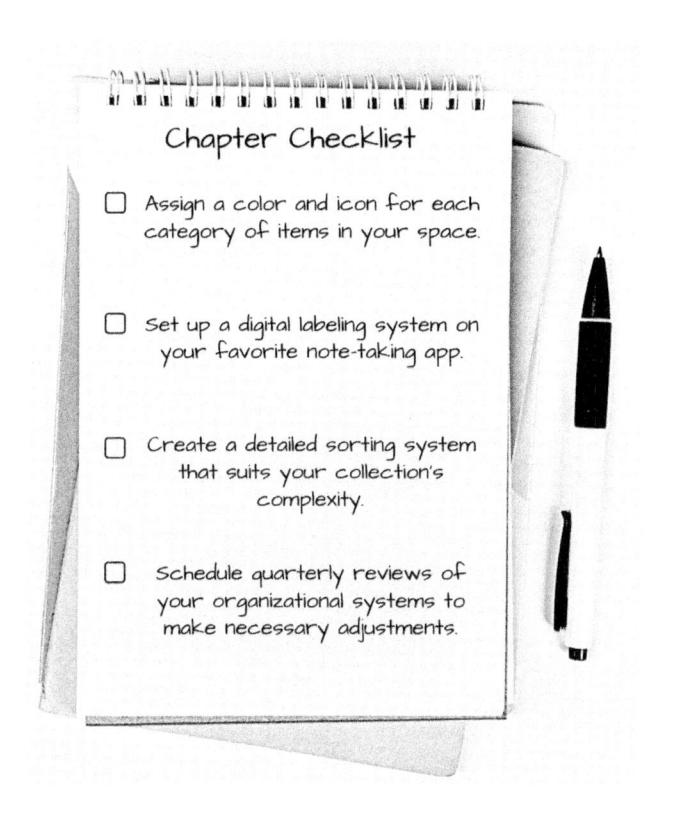

> **Chapter Checklist**
>
> ☐ Assign a color and icon for each category of items in your space.
>
> ☐ Set up a digital labeling system on your favorite note-taking app.
>
> ☐ Create a detailed sorting system that suits your collection's complexity.
>
> ☐ Schedule quarterly reviews of your organizational systems to make necessary adjustments.

Bullet Point Summary

- Use color coding and visual tags for efficient sorting.
- Implement electronic labeling systems for ease and consistency.
- Develop multi-layered sorting systems for complex collections.
- Conduct regular reviews to keep your system functional and up-to-date.

PART IX

LONG-TERM SUCCESS AND CONTINUOUS IMPROVEMENT

Imagine you're a juggler at the circus; your organizational tools and strategies are the brightly colored pins you keep effortlessly swirling through the air. Now, what happens when the show ends, the tent is packed, and it's time for the next town? You'd review your performance, tweak your throws, maybe add a new pin or two, right? That's precisely what we're diving into in this chapter —keeping your organizational game not just running but evolving and exciting long after the initial setup thrill has calmed down.

CHAPTER 9.1

REVIEWING AND REVISING YOUR ORGANIZATIONAL SYSTEMS

So, you've set up systems that once felt as refreshing as a new season of your favorite series. But just like any series that starts to lose its charm around season 4, your systems might need a bit of a plot twist. This is where scheduled reviews come into play. Imagine setting up a calendar alert named 'Organizational Tune-up'—because, let's be honest, we all need a little nudge. This isn't just a reminder but a cue to hit pause in your bustling life and check in with your systems. How frequently? Well, think of it like a dental check-up: not exactly the highlight of your week, but skipping it leads to more problems than you want to deal with. Quarterly reviews hit that sweet spot—just enough to catch snags without making you feel like you're stuck in a never-ending rerun of organizing.

But what exactly are you looking for in these reviews? Here's where your criteria for revision come into play. Picture this: Each part of your system is up for an audition, showcasing how well it has performed since the last review. You're the judge, and you're looking for three things: ease of use (because no one needs extra complications), effectiveness in reducing stress (because peace of mind is the goal), and alignment with your current goals (because static systems in a dynamic life? No thanks). If any part of your system isn't making the cut, it might be time to switch things up.

Now, if the thought of making changes makes you feel like you're redoing everything from scratch, let's talk about iterative improvement. It's about minor adjustments, not sweeping reforms—no need to Marie Kondo your entire life in one weekend! Think of it as fine-tuning a recipe—sometimes, all you need is a pinch of salt to take your dish from "meh" to "wow." Minor tweaks can lead to significant improvements without the overwhelming stress of a complete overhaul.

Feedback is your friend here—and not just any feedback, but structured insights from those who see your organizational efforts in action—family, friends, or even colleagues. Set up a simple form, or just ask them over coffee, "Hey, how do you find the new layout in the living room?" or "Is finding files easier with the new digital system?" This isn't just about validation; it's about actionable insights that can steer your next small yet impactful tweak.

In this ongoing show of life, where you're constantly juggling roles and responsibilities, think of these scheduled reviews and iterative improvements as your rehearsal times. I know it can feel overwhelming trying to keep all the balls in the air, but remember, you're doing a fantastic job. Taking the time to pause and adjust doesn't mean you're slowing down; it means you're making your performance even more spectacular. They're your chance to refine your performance, making sure that each juggling pin is dazzling enough to keep the show spectacular and, most importantly, that it feels magical to you, the headliner of this beautiful whirlwind of a circus. Keep shining—you've got this, and I'm cheering you on every step of the way!

CHAPTER 9.1 | 307

Chapter Checklist

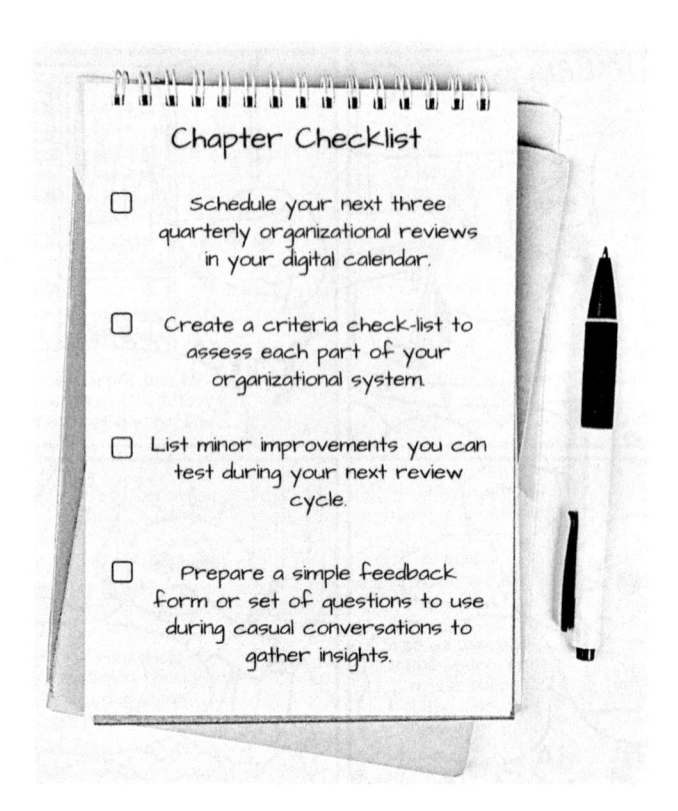

- [ ] Schedule your next three quarterly organizational reviews in your digital calendar.

- [ ] Create a criteria check-list to assess each part of your organizational system.

- [ ] List minor improvements you can test during your next review cycle.

- [ ] Prepare a simple feedback form or set of questions to use during casual conversations to gather insights.

Bullet Point Summary

- Set quarterly review reminders to assess and tune your organizational systems.
- Evaluate each system's ease of use, stress reduction effectiveness, and goal alignment.
- Implement minor, iterative improvements rather than complete overhauls.
- Seek and utilize structured feedback from your personal community to guide enhancements.

CHAPTER 9.2

STAYING MOTIVATED: LONG-TERM STRATEGIES FOR ORGANIZATIONAL SUCCESS

Imagine this: you've just nailed the perfect system, and everything's organized, from your spice rack to your digital files, feeling like a freshly minted coin—shiny and full of promise. But as days slip into weeks, the shine starts to dull. The old chaos, like an uninvited house guest, begins creeping back. So, how do you keep the momentum? How do you ensure that your organizational system doesn't just work for now but keeps working, evolving, and thriving? The secret sauce is in staying motivated, continuously setting fresh goals, and keeping the rewards sweet and the support strong.

Let's kick off with setting new goals. It's like setting waypoints on a long trek. Each one gives you a burst of achievement and a fresh viewpoint (plus, you don't get lost wondering how you ended up deep-diving into an IKEA catalog instead of decluttering). Start with what you've already accomplished and map out where you want to go next. These goals should be like Goldilocks—not too hard, not too easy, just right. Achievable goals prevent the demotivation of constant failure, while realistic challenges keep boredom at bay (because we all know boredom is an ADHD kryptonite). And here's a pro tip: break those goals down. If your goal is to organize your entire home, start with one drawer, then a closet, then a room. Each small victory is a step towards the grand prize, and every step is a boost to keep going—like finding a hidden $5 in your jeans pocket, but, you know, for your whole house.

Now, have you ever thought of creating a vision board for your organizational goals? Here's why you should: it's a visual pep-talk. This isn't just about slapping pictures on a board; it's about crafting a visual narrative of what you want to achieve and what that achievement looks like. Whether it's pictures of a clutter-free home office or snapshots of your neatly filed digital photos, make it a collage of your aspirations. Place it somewhere you'll see daily. This isn't just décor; it's your daily dose of inspiration, a reminder of where you're heading, and the beautiful view along the way.

Rewards, oh sweet rewards, how crucial you are! Setting up a personal reward system is like giving yourself a high-five (or a mental fist bump for adulting). Each time you hit a small goal or stick to your system for a week, reward yourself. Maybe it's a night out, a new book, or a guilt-free Netflix binge where you don't have to convince yourself *just one more episode* is totally fine. These rewards create a positive link in your brain between staying organized and feeling good. It turns what might sometimes feel like a slog into a series of celebrations. Life's too short not to celebrate—especially when you finally remember where you put that missing sock!

Don't underestimate the power of community support. Whether it's a local group or an online forum, find your tribe. These are the folks who cheer you on when you're up and give you a push when you're down. They're the ones who share their successes and their face-palm moments. Join or form a group focused on organization

—share tips, vent about setbacks, and celebrate wins together. It's about turning the solitary act of organizing into a communal journey of improvement, learning, and, yes, a bit of commiserating.

By embracing these strategies, you're not just maintaining an organizational system; you're nurturing a lifestyle of clarity, purpose, and joy. I know the path of organization is never a straight line—it's more like trying to follow a GPS that keeps saying, "Recalculating route." But with each step reviewed, each goal set, each success celebrated, and each lesson shared, you're more than just organized—you're invigorated, motivated, and ever-evolving. So keep setting those goals, pinning those dreams, and cherishing the rewards and community that make the journey worthwhile. You've got this, and I'm cheering you on every step of the way!

312 | EFFORTLESS ADHD ORGANIZATION

Chapter Checklist

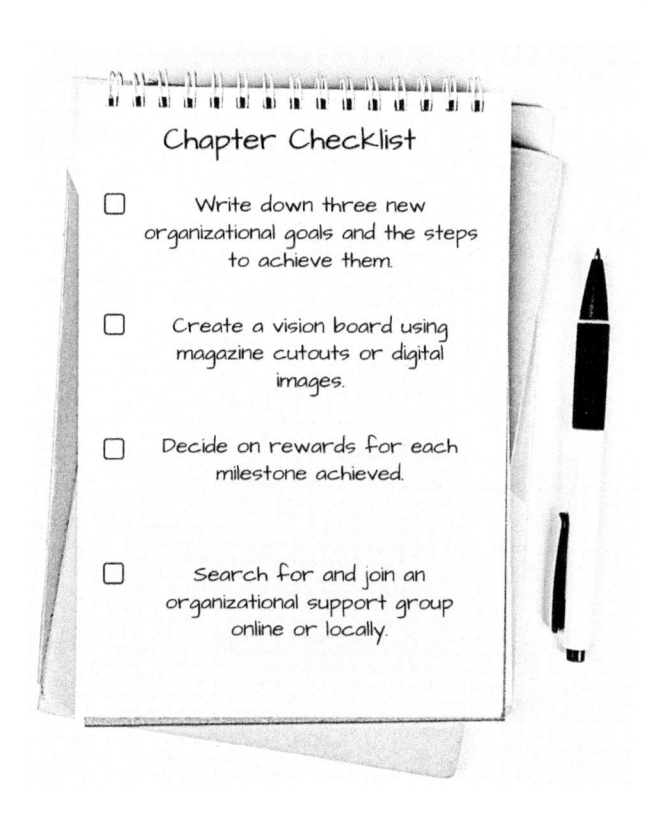

☐ Write down three new organizational goals and the steps to achieve them.

☐ Create a vision board using magazine cutouts or digital images.

☐ Decide on rewards for each milestone achieved.

☐ Search for and join an organizational support group online or locally.

Bullet Point Summary

- Continuously set new, achievable, and slightly challenging goals.
- Create and update a vision board to keep your aspirations visual and present.
- Establish a personal reward system to make staying organized enjoyable.
- Engage with community groups for support, motivation, and shared learning.

CHAPTER 9.3

EMBRACING NEW ORGANIZATIONAL TECHNOLOGIES AND TOOLS

Let's face it: keeping up with the latest gadgets and apps can feel like trying to sip water from a fire hose—overwhelming, messy, yet somehow exciting. For those of us navigating the vibrant landscapes of ADHD, diving into the latest organizational tools can seem like a double-edged sword. Yes, they promise a world of streamlined processes and simplified tasks. Yet, they can also add to the pile of underused apps sitting in our digital graveyard, right next to that yoga app we downloaded but never opened. Yet, the right approach to embracing new technologies can turn them from potential clutter to powerful allies in our quest for organized living.

First off, staying updated doesn't mean you need to jump on every tech trend that pops up on your Twitter feed. Instead, think of it as being a selective curator for your own museum of organizational tools. Subscribe to a couple of reliable tech blogs or follow thought leaders who resonate with your needs. The goal here is to keep your finger on the pulse of new technologies without allowing them to overwhelm you. Think of it as window shopping—you're just keeping an eye out for that perfect tool that could really make a difference, not buying out the store.

Now, when you do spot that shiny new app or gadget that promises to be the next big thing in organization, how do you approach it? Experimentation is critical, but it's the careful kind—not the "let's rearrange everything at 2 AM and hope for the best" kind. Start small. If it's an app, try it with a few non-critical tasks to see how it holds up. Does it integrate well with your existing tools, or is it just another pretty icon taking up space on your phone? This phase is crucial; it's about testing the waters before you cannonball into the deep end of another digital rabbit hole.

Integrating new tools into your existing system is a bit like introducing a new kitten to your old cat—the introduction needs to be gradual and sensitive. If you decide the tool is a keeper, start by integrating it into less complex areas of your organization system. Watch how it interacts with your other tools. Is it the cooperative type, enhancing your existing setup, or does it start knocking things off the shelves, causing chaos? Smooth transitions are all about compatibility and complementing your established routines, not overturning them.

Evaluating the effectiveness of new technology is where you go from being a curious user to a sharp-eyed critic like Gordon Ramsay but with fewer expletives (hopefully). Here's where you need to be brutally honest with yourself. Has this tool actually saved you time, or is it just another fancy way to procrastinate? Has it reduced your stress or added another layer of digital chaos to your routine? Sometimes, what looks brilliant in advertisements might work as well as trying to organize your life with a broken pencil. Track how you interact with it over a few weeks. Note any significant changes in productivity or if it's just another app collecting virtual dust. After all, the goal is to make life easier, not just to impress your phone with new downloads!

In this dynamic digital age, where the only constant is change, adapting and evolving your organizational toolkit isn't just helpful; it's essential. I know it can sometimes feel overwhelming with so many new tools and apps vying for your attention, but give yourself credit for being open to exploring what works best for you. Remember, it's perfectly okay to take your time and choose what truly fits your needs. By staying informed, experimenting cautiously, integrating wisely, and evaluating critically, you ensure that your organizational system remains robust, responsive, and remarkably in tune with your needs. So, go ahead, dip your toes into the waters of new technology—you might just find the perfect wave to ride to organizational success. You've got this, and I'm cheering you on every step of the way!

318 | EFFORTLESS ADHD ORGANIZATION

Chapter Checklist

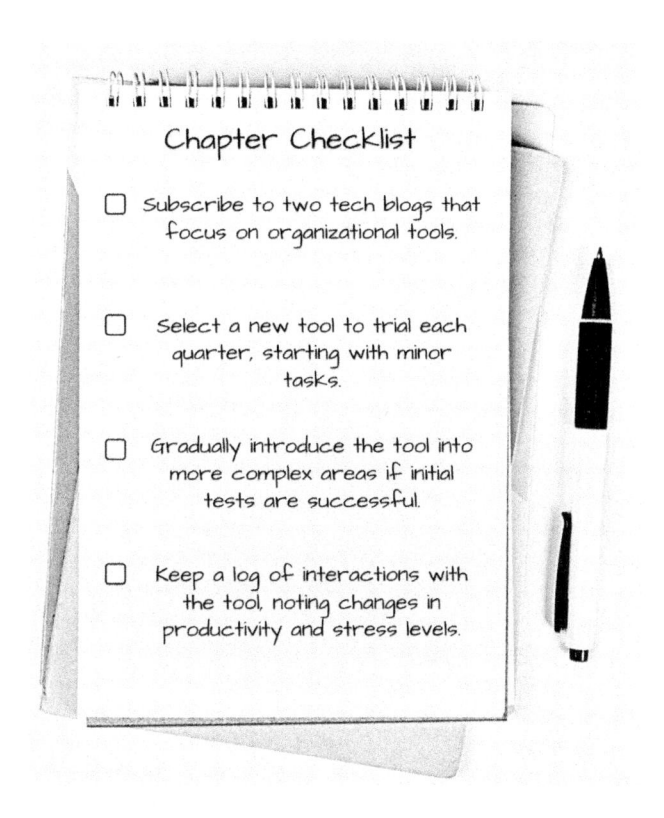

- ☐ Subscribe to two tech blogs that focus on organizational tools.

- ☐ Select a new tool to trial each quarter, starting with minor tasks.

- ☐ Gradually introduce the tool into more complex areas if initial tests are successful.

- ☐ Keep a log of interactions with the tool, noting changes in productivity and stress levels.

Bullet Point Summary

- Stay updated by following select tech blogs and influencers.
- Experiment with new tools on a small scale before full integration.
- Gradually integrate successful tools into your broader system.
- Critically evaluate new tools based on time efficiency and stress reduction.

CHAPTER 9.4

DEALING WITH SETBACKS AND REORGANIZING

It's like you're on a roll, cruising down your organizational highway, tunes blaring, wind in your hair, and then—bam! You hit a pothole. Perhaps it's a missed deadline, a lost document, or suddenly, your meticulously organized spice rack (alphabetized and all) becomes a jumbled mess thanks to a well-meaning toddler. Setbacks in your organizational efforts are not just bumps on the road; sometimes, they feel like full-on roadblocks. But here's the kicker: recognizing these setbacks early can be like having a GPS that reroutes you before you're way off course.

Recognizing setbacks isn't about beating yourself up; it's about tuning in to the early warning signals. Maybe it's the stress that's creeping up, making you snap at your partner over misplaced keys, or the third time this month you've double-booked yourself. These signs are your early warning system, telling you it's time to pull over and check your organizational map. It's about acknowledging, without judgment, that what worked yesterday might not be working today. And that's okay! Change isn't just part of life; it's the core of growth—even in your organizational systems.

Now, how do you move past these setbacks? First, take a step back. This isn't defeat; it's a strategic retreat—like pulling over to recheck your GPS after missing the same turn twice. Look at your goals and the systems you've set up. Maybe they need a little tweaking. It's like adjusting your sails when the wind changes direction—not a sign of failure, just a necessary part of navigating. If a system or tool isn't serving you as it used to, ask yourself why. Could that fancy digital tool be swapped out for something simpler? Is your schedule looking more like a Tetris game with no empty spaces? Sometimes, overcoming setbacks means revising your goals to better align with your current reality—a reality that acknowledges both your ambitions and your well-being.

Learning from these hiccups is crucial. Every missed deadline has a story to tell; every bit of feedback from those around you holds insights. Maybe it's discovering that you're more productive in the mornings, so shifting your deep-focus tasks to that time could prevent future project delays. Or perhaps it's realizing that your phone is a vortex of distraction during work hours, leading you to set boundaries that keep your focus sharp. Each mistake is a lesson dressed in disguise, waiting to be unraveled and understood, not feared.

Building resilience is your secret weapon here. It's not about armoring yourself against setbacks—none of us are superheroes with capes (though a cape would be fun)—it's about weaving a safety net that catches you when you inevitably trip over that invisible obstacle called life. This resilience comes from maintaining a positive outlook, seeing setbacks as temporary and totally conquerable, like a speed bump on the road to greatness (hopefully not the end-all "German speedbump," though). It also comes from stress-relief practices. Whether it's yoga, meditation, or that weekly movie night where you rewatch the same comedy for the 12th time because it's your "comfort zone," find what refills your cup and make it part of your routine. This isn't an indulgence—it's essential maintenance for your well-being.

Navigating setbacks isn't about never falling; it's about learning how to land softer and get back up faster. It's about refining your systems, understanding your needs, and fortifying your resilience. I know it's not always easy, and sometimes it feels like the road is full of obstacles, but remember that every bump is a chance to grow and learn. You've come so far already, and your strength shines through every challenge you overcome. So next time you hit a pothole, remember, it's just part of the journey—one that you're more than equipped to navigate with a bit of creativity, a lot of self-compassion, and an unyielding commitment to personal growth. Keep believing in yourself—give yourself some grace, and I'm here cheering you on every step of the way!

324 | EFFORTLESS ADHD ORGANIZATION

Chapter Checklist

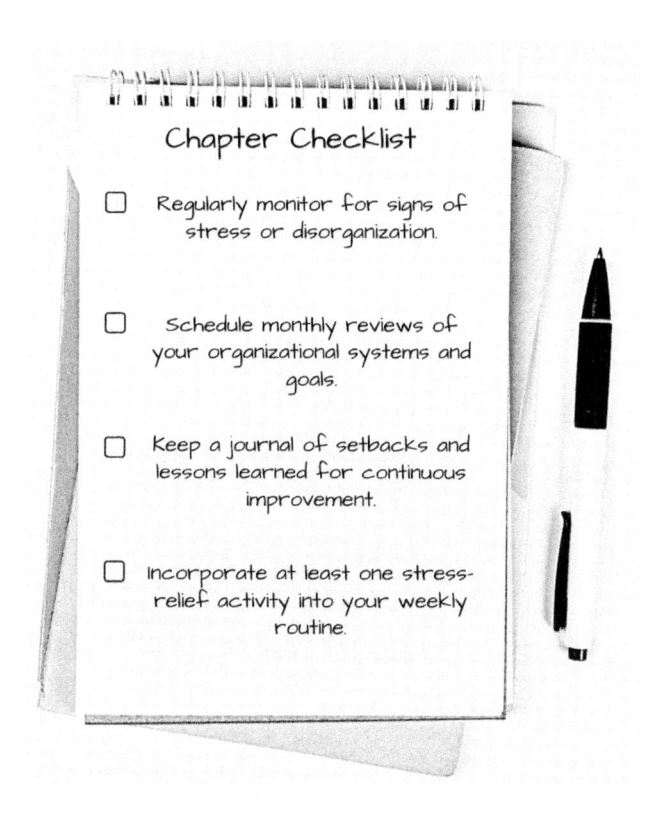

- ☐ Regularly monitor for signs of stress or disorganization.

- ☐ Schedule monthly reviews of your organizational systems and goals.

- ☐ Keep a journal of setbacks and lessons learned for continuous improvement.

- ☐ Incorporate at least one stress-relief activity into your weekly routine.

Bullet Point Summary

- Tune into early signs of setbacks like increased stress or recurring mistakes.
- Revisit and adjust your goals and systems as needed to realign with current needs.
- View each mistake as a learning opportunity that offers valuable insights.
- Invest in building resilience through positive outlooks and regular stress-relief activities.

CHAPTER 9.5

CELEBRATING YOUR ORGANIZATIONAL ACHIEVEMENTS

Imagine you've just crossed the finish line of your local marathon—not just any marathon, but one you've trained for amidst a chaotic schedule, balancing work, home, and possibly even searching for those keys you swore you left in the *same* spot every time. You wouldn't just grab your medal and casually walk off, right? Nope, you'd bask in the glory, snap some pics, and probably post about it. Well, think of each milestone in your organizational journey as that finish line. Celebrating these wins isn't just a nice pat on the back; it's your victory lap—fueling the next round of chaos-taming greatness, keeping the momentum alive and kicking!

Let's talk about the importance of recognizing these achievements. You see, every time you acknowledge a job well done, be it finally sorting out that dreaded junk drawer or mastering your weekly meal prep, you're reinforcing positive behavior. It's about telling your brain, "Hey, that felt good! Let's do it again." This celebration creates a feedback loop that not only enhances your motivation but also deepens the satisfaction you derive from being organized.

It transforms your efforts from mundane tasks into victories worth striving for again and again.

Now, how about keeping a success journal? Think of it as your personal highlight reel—except instead of ESPN showing your best slam dunks, it's filled with your most satisfying clutter-conquering moments. This isn't just any journal; it's like a trophy case for all your wins and the strategies that got you there. Each entry is a reminder that, yes, you *can* organize that drawer (even if it did take three tries). Start by jotting down today's date, what you organized, how you did it, and most importantly, how it made you feel—probably something between "I did it!" and "I never want to see another cord tangle again." This practice will keep your achievements fresh and serve as your go-to pep talk when the clutter tries to stage a comeback.

Sharing your successes brings a whole new level of joy. Whether it's showing before-and-after photos of your pantry on social media or just telling a friend about how you've finally nailed your filing system, sharing invites celebration and support from your community. It turns your personal victories into collective celebrations. You might even inspire someone else to tackle their organizational challenges, spreading the ripple effect of your achievements.

And why not wrap up each year with an annual review celebration? Picture it—an excuse for a party where, instead of small talk, people swap their best organizational hacks (and maybe you finally figure out where those mystery chargers actually belong). Or keep it simple with a quiet evening reflecting over your success journal, where you can pat yourself on the back for finally organizing that junk drawer you swore you'd get to three years ago. It's about closing the year on a high note, celebrating the progress you've made, and setting the tone for the year ahead. Plus, who doesn't want to enter a new year feeling like they've already won?

As you weave these practices into your life, each small victory adds a stitch to the rich tapestry of your organizational journey. I know that sometimes it might feel like you're trying to organize a whirlwind—after all, managing ADHD is no small feat! But with every achievement celebrated and every success shared, you're not just organizing your space—you're enriching your life. I'm so proud of how you're turning challenges into triumphs, crafting a narrative of progress that propels you forward, one joyful victory at a time. Keep embracing each moment with that incredible spirit—you've got this!

330 | EFFORTLESS ADHD ORGANIZATION

Chapter Checklist

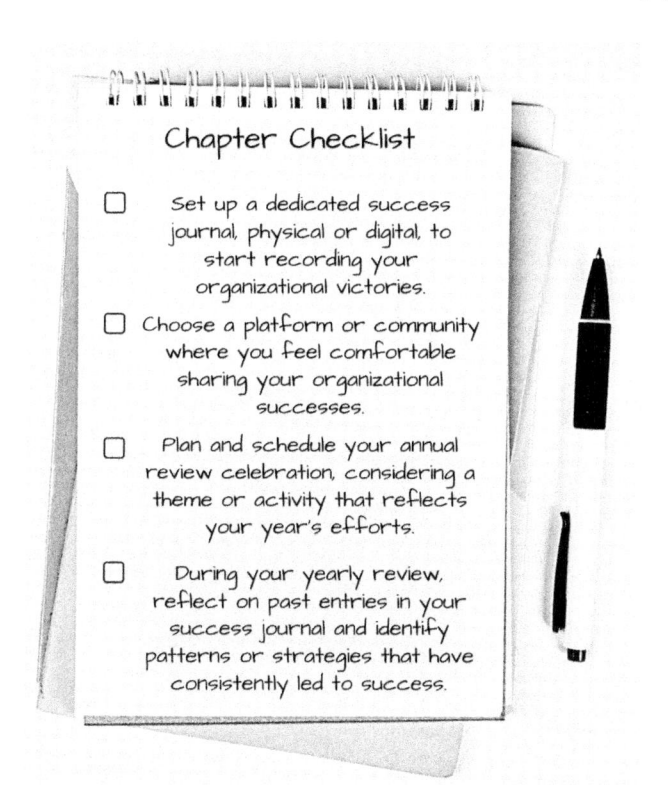

- [ ] Set up a dedicated success journal, physical or digital, to start recording your organizational victories.

- [ ] Choose a platform or community where you feel comfortable sharing your organizational successes.

- [ ] Plan and schedule your annual review celebration, considering a theme or activity that reflects your year's efforts.

- [ ] During your yearly review, reflect on past entries in your success journal and identify patterns or strategies that have consistently led to success.

Bullet Point Summary

- Recognize and celebrate every organizational achievement, no matter the size.
- Maintain a success journal to document and reflect on your organizational victories and effective strategies.
- Share your successes with friends, family, or online communities to multiply the joy and inspire others.
- Conduct an annual review celebration to reflect on past achievements and set goals for the future.

CHAPTER 9.6

FUTURE-PROOFING YOUR ORGANIZATION SKILLS

Adapting to life changes—new careers, moving house, or shifts in family dynamics—can sometimes feel like you're trying to repaint your house while it's still on fire. It's hectic, it's hot, and heck, it's sometimes all too much. But that's where the beauty of adaptable organizational skills comes into play. Think of your organizational system as your personal toolkit, not just filled with tools but with Swiss Army knives—versatile, adaptable, and always ready for whatever life throws at you.

Let's start with the big moves—maybe you're scaling up your career, moving to a new city, or welcoming a new member to your family. Each of these life events doesn't just pack a punch on your personal life; they send ripples through your organizational systems as well. Preparing for these changes involves a proactive approach. For example, if you're moving to a new house, begin by mentally mapping out the space. Where will your existing organizational systems fit? What adjustments will you need? Perhaps the new kitchen has fewer cabinets, or the home office is now also a guest room. Adjust your system by predicting where you'll need to tighten up or expand your storage solutions. Use floor plans or even a simple sketch to start reimagining your spaces. It's like directing your life's play before the curtain rises—anticipate the scene changes and prepare accordingly.

Now, while the stage is set for change, continuous skill development ensures you're constantly sharpening your tools, ready to carve out success no matter the wood you're working with. Engaging in ongoing learning—attending workshops, reading up on the latest in productivity, or even signing up for online courses—keeps you at the top of your game. Think of it like leveling up in a video game, except instead of earning powers, you're gaining the ability to organize your life like a pro (and maybe find those car keys you lost for the third time this week). Each new skill is a stepping stone, not just for your career but for maintaining and enhancing your organizational superpowers, turning chaos into order with just a flick of your newfound knowledge.

Anticipating future needs is about staying two steps ahead. Just like a chess player, you need to think beyond the next move. Start by assessing your life's possible trajectories and consider the organizational challenges each may present. Are you planning to work more remotely? You might need a more robust digital organization system. Considering starting a family? Think about how baby gear, schedules, and family paperwork will fit into your current setup. This foresight allows you to tweak your systems incrementally, preventing the need for a complete overhaul when life inevitably evolves.

Sustainability in organization is about the long game; it's making sure that your systems do not just survive but thrive—kind of like trying to keep a houseplant alive, except with fewer mysterious brown leaves. This could mean opting for digital tools that reduce paper waste or investing in high-quality, reusable organizing supplies that stand the test of time. Sustainability is also about your systems' ability to sustain your growing and ever-changing life (because, let's be honest, ADHD doesn't exactly keep things static). It's a commitment to making your organizational habits both environmentally and personally sustainable, ensuring that as your life evolves, your systems grow with it—seamlessly and, ideally, with a little less clutter.

Navigating through life's changes with an adaptable, skill-enhanced, anticipatory, and sustainable organizational approach not only smooths out the bumps but turns them into ramps, propelling you forward faster and more prepared than ever. I know that embracing change isn't always easy, but your ability to adapt and grow is truly remarkable. You've tackled challenges head-on and have transformed them into opportunities for success. Remember, every step you take is a testament to your strength and resilience. Whether it's a new baby, a new home, or a new job, with your organizational toolkit by your side, you're ready to take on the world—one beautifully organized step at a time.

336 | EFFORTLESS ADHD ORGANIZATION

Chapter Checklist

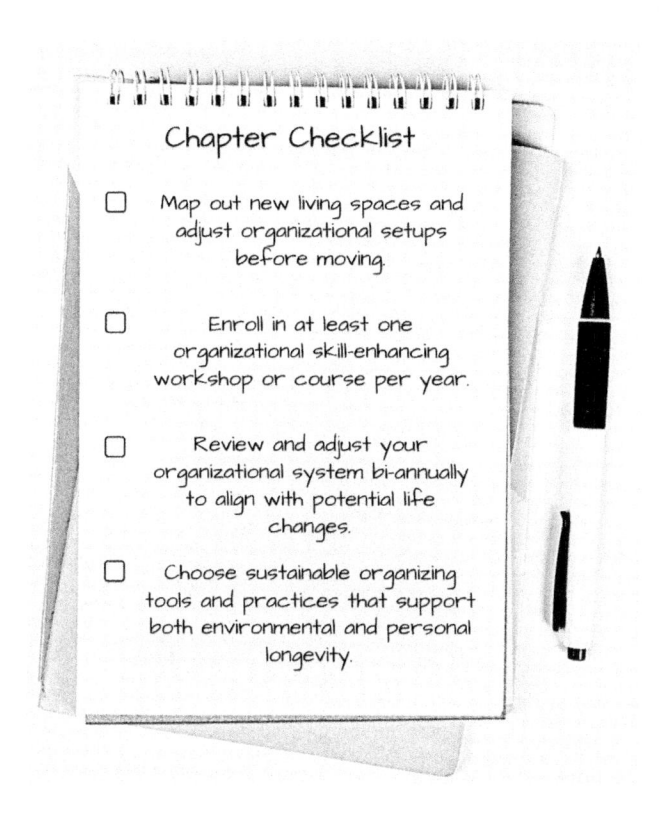

- [ ] Map out new living spaces and adjust organizational setups before moving.

- [ ] Enroll in at least one organizational skill-enhancing workshop or course per year.

- [ ] Review and adjust your organizational system bi-annually to align with potential life changes.

- [ ] Choose sustainable organizing tools and practices that support both environmental and personal longevity.

Bullet Point Summary

- Proactively adapt systems in anticipation of major life changes.
- Continuously develop organizational skills through learning opportunities.
- Stay ahead by anticipating future needs and adjusting systems accordingly.
- Invest in sustainable practices for long-term organizational success.

'TILL WE MEET AGAIN

Well, here we are at the end of our shared journey through the maze of ADHD-specific organization. Together, we've tackled the whirlwinds of clutter—both physical and digital—and discovered strategies that not only manage our unique brains but also celebrate them. From embracing visual aids to mastering the art of short, manageable tasks, this book has been a toolkit tailored to harness the vivid, sometimes chaotic, always extraordinary world of living with ADHD.

Living with ADHD is undeniably challenging, but as we've explored these pages, we've also seen it's brimming with potential. Each strategy we've discussed isn't just a method for organization; it's a step towards empowerment. It's about turning what many see as hurdles into launchpads for success, allowing us to live a life that's not just organized but is genuinely fulfilling.

Remember, the essence of these strategies is flexibility. Whether you're a student juggling deadlines, a professional climbing the career ladder, or a parent managing a household, these techniques are your clay—mold them in ways that best suit your vibrant, dynamic lifestyle. Adaptation is vital, and personalizing these strategies will make them all the more effective.

I cannot stress enough the importance of self-compassion and patience on this journey. Organizing your life with ADHD is a marathon, not a sprint. Celebrate the small victories, learn from the setbacks, and treat yourself with kindness along the way. You're doing more than organizing your space and time; you're building a foundation for long-term well-being.

As you move forward, keep your mind open to new ideas, tools, and insights that can aid your organizational endeavors. The world evolves, and so do our lives and needs. Staying curious and adaptable will ensure that your organizational systems grow and change with you.

I encourage you to connect with others on this path. There are communities out there, both online and in the real world, filled with individuals who share your experiences. Engage with these groups. Share your stories, your successes, and, yes, even your struggles. There's strength in numbers and immense comfort in knowing you're not navigating this path alone.

And speaking of sharing, I would love to hear from you. How have the strategies in this book worked for your unique situation? Your stories are the wind beneath the wings of this ongoing project. Share them on social media and forums, or drop me a message directly. Let's keep the conversation going.

As we part ways in this book, I leave you with this: Believe in your ability to harness your ADHD in ways that bring out your best. With organization as your ally, there's no limit to what you can achieve. Approach each day with resilience, a dash of humor, and an open heart. You have the tools; now go build the life you dream of.

Finally, don't forget the plethora of resources we've discussed—apps, websites, and tools that are there to support you as you refine your organizational systems. Use them as your compass in the ever-exciting quest for clarity and organization.

Thank you for trusting me on this remarkable journey. Your commitment to turning the pages of this book is a testament to your commitment to enhancing your life. Don't treat this book as a one-and-done experience; remember, the difference between the apprentice and the master is "the master has failed more times than the apprentice has even tried" --Stephen McCranie. Reread this book, and again, and again...just like the master who tries over and over...and someday soon--through this book and your hard work--you'll be able to teach others after having mastered yourself. Here's to organized spaces, clear minds, and vibrant, fulfilling lives. Keep soaring high, and remember, in the world of ADHD, organized chaos isn't just a possibility—it's a superpower!

If this book changed a single aspect of your life for the better, please share it with others and, if you're willing, leave me an honest review on Amazon. My goal is to make ADHD more navigable for everyone, one life at a time; with your help, I know we can do it!

KEEPING THE GAME ALIVE

"We make a living by what we get, but we make a life by what we give."

— WINSTON CHURCHILL

Now that you've got everything you need to tackle ADHD organization and streamline your life, it's time to pass on your newfound knowledge and help others who are just getting started.

By simply leaving your honest opinion of *Effortless ADHD Organization* on Amazon, you'll guide other adults with ADHD to the same tools that helped you. Your review could be the reason someone else finds the information they desperately need to take control of their life and reduce the chaos.

Thank you for your help. The journey of mastering ADHD organization continues when we share what we've learned—and you're helping to keep that knowledge alive.

Scan the QR code to leave your review on Amazon.

With all the love & gratitude,

Sterling Cheney

REFERENCES

Small Space, Big Impact: The Art of Organization and Decluttering – Talento Design. https://talentodesign.ca/small-space-big-impact-the-art-of-organization-and-decluttering/

Printed in Dunstable, United Kingdom